SHIPWRECK ON THE POTOMAC

DISASTER IN PURSUIT OF LINCOLN'S KILLER

KAREN E. STONE

Published by The History Press
An imprint of Arcadia Publishing
Charleston, SC
www.historypress.com

Back cover painting by Angela M. Wathen.

First published 2025

Manufactured in the United States

ISBN 9781467158671

Library of Congress Control Number: 2025931729

CONTENTS

Contents

ACKNOWLEDGEMENTS

Authors always say that there are too many people to thank, and I now understand what they mean. There are far too many individuals who answered my emails and took my phone calls in libraries, archives and museums up and down the East Coast to list them all. But that does not mean they are any less appreciated nor that their help is any less important. To name just a few, Michael J. Brewer, NOAA archivist for Historical Environmental Information, provided invaluable information on the night sky, the tides and other important information about the environment in April 1865. The staff at the National Archives were wonderful, answering questions and digging out records over and over again for me. And I must also mention the staff of the Steamship Historical Society of America, who found the image of the *Massachusetts* for me. The Leonardtown Library served as one of my favorite places to write, and I appreciate the staff allowing me to spend hours working in their beautiful lobby. There are many friends and colleagues without whose encouragement, trust and belief in me this would not have been possible. I thank them all most sincerely.

But there are some whom I would like to mention by name. The first person is Chris Howland, who got this entire project started by telling me to write the story myself, not rely on him or some other magazine writer to do it for me. And so, it began. I wrote the article; it was published, and now here is the fleshed-out version. It is not complete; there are still some unanswered questions, but to quote my husband, "Getting the story out there is more important than answering every single question."

I must also thank Drew Gruber, of Civil War Trails, who provided the opportunity for me to meet Chris and whose masterful storytelling skills have been inspiring to say the least. Abi Lyn Voss fits into this category of supporters as well, for having nearly completed the work, I was stalling in sending it off to a publisher. But she convinced me there was no shame in being turned down a time or two, so I submitted it, and lo and behold, it was accepted on my first try! Catherine Wienraub, Dave Heiby and the other historians in Alexandria also went above and beyond in sharing information and maps, digging into records even after I left the building and generally being supportive. And they are helping to tell this story through their talks and tours there. My thanks go also to Kate Jenkins at The History Press for seeing the value in the story, walking me through the early process and then placing me in the capable hands of John Rodrigue, who has been nothing but encouraging, helpful and patient in seeing this process through.

I would also like to thank Don Cropp for introducing me to the story in the first place, and Donald G. Shomette, my favorite local author who answered so many questions, shared information while he was doing his research and was so encouraging about everything from the very start. And it was he who introduced me to David Howe and the group at the Institute of Maritime History. Not only was David and the *Roper* crew looking for the *Black Diamond*'s remains on the bottom of the river, but David was also willing to share much of his knowledge of maritime law with me. And when I needed further explanation and help, Molly Fleury and Buffy Giddens, two other attorney friends, came to my rescue.

A huge thank-you goes out to local artist Angela M. Wathen, who as soon as she heard the story immediately painted a rendition of the accident and gifted it to the St. Clement's Island Museum. There are no known depictions of the event of any kind, so having a visual to accompany the story was a true gift. Not being satisfied with just one, she went on to create two others. The first painting is included within the book.

All of my colleagues in St. Mary's County have been amazingly patient and supportive. They have listened to hours of my talking about this incident, have read countless renditions of various chapters and have been my biggest cheerleaders. Special thanks go to Jenna Guzman for seeing the value of this project on so many levels and for immediately putting together a marketing plan, complete with a launch party. And to Andrew Ponti, who so generously read and reread the manuscript, pointing out sentences that contained a passive voice, catching misplaced and missing commas and generally teaching me all those English grammar lessons I never learned in school. You have all been amazing.

But my biggest champion and the one to whom I owe the most is my husband—William E. Stone. He is my walking Civil War dictionary, my traveling companion, my photographer, my decipherer of nineteenth-century handwriting and signatures and my "explainer of all things military." I am grateful for his patience, for his encouragement and for his continued presence at my side as we travel down this rocky road that is life.

INTRODUCTION

It has always been said that not a single life was lost during the hunt for John Wilkes Booth. This is said with pride, as it should be. If only it were true.

In the 1860s, life on the Potomac River was quite different than it is today. Instead of the calm, open waters, the river was the frontline of battle. The Potomac was the main lifeline out of Washington, D.C., and for the federal government, it was the dividing line between the warring sections of the North and South. For the people of St. Mary's County, Maryland, the most southern point on Maryland's western shore, just across the Potomac River from Confederate Virginia, it was the source of their livelihood and much of their food; and for some, it became their final resting place. This is a story of that river and of the men whose lives were lost in the aftermath of the Civil War in the hunt for the presidential assassin John Wilkes Booth. These men had answered the call of the president to serve their country and had survived battles and hardships in the field and at prison camps, but they couldn't survive this disaster. This work is for those eighty-seven men who lost their lives in the shipwreck between *Black Diamond* and *Massachusetts* so that they will no longer be forgotten, because a *man is only missing if he is forgotten.*

All the place names in this work are those current in 1865. When quoting letters, telegrams and other period documents, the original spellings and punctuation have been retained, as much as possible. The only changes made were for the sake of clarity.

CHAPTER I

MARYLAND AT THE TIME

The Department is informed that Mr. Plunkett, at Leonardtown, MD, has boats which he uses to convey news and rebels from Maryland to Virginia.
—Navy Department telegram, September 25, 1862, from Gideon Welles, secretary of the navy, to Commodore Andrew A. Harwood, U.S. Navy, Commanding Potomac Flotilla

For Southern Marylanders, trade, communication and even marriages had been focused on Virginia's Northern Neck for centuries. For them, it was much closer and more accessible than most places in Maryland. The working men of both states shared the waters of the Potomac, working side by side, getting to know each other and finding that they shared sympathies and the desire to avoid involvement in national affairs. None of this changed with the outbreak of the Civil War.

On April 12, 1861, Fort Sumter was fired on. President Abraham Lincoln issued a call to arms on the fifteenth, and the governments in the border states now needed to choose a side. On April 18, the *St. Mary's Beacon* newspaper reported that when the intelligence that Fort Sumter had surrendered was received, the "wildest enthusiasm broke forth among our [Leonardtown] people, and huzzahs and congratulations and rejoicings were the order of the hour. The bells rang a merry peal, and [Riley's] Rifles fired several volleys in honor of the event." Maryland's governor, Thomas Holliday Hicks, refused to answer Lincoln's call. He wrote to Secretary of War Simon Cameron that the organized military forces in Baltimore were for the South and had taken possession of the armories and so had all the arms and ammunition, so "I therefore think it prudent to decline (for the present) responding affirmatively to the requisition made by President Lincoln for four regiments of infantry."[1]

On April 17, Virginia declared that it would leave the Union, which made Maryland essential to the defenses of Washington, D.C. (Although the decision was made on April 17, Virginia did not actually become part of the Confederacy until May 23.) Confederate batteries began to line the shores of the Potomac River on the Virginia side after the Battle of First Manassas, creating a virtual blockade of the river and putting an end to steamship travel on the Virginia side. Ships that did continue to run stopped only on the Maryland shores (Maryland owns the entire river, up to the high tide line on the Virginia shore), but the U.S. Navy ultimately told ships not to use the Potomac for fear of capture or destruction. This cut off the primary Federal supply line, causing ships to have to travel to Baltimore, unload their goods onto railroad cars and then proceed to Washington, D.C. If Maryland voted to secede, the railroad supply line would also be closed, and the Federal capital would be surrounded by hostile lands.

On April 19, riots broke out in Baltimore between Confederate sympathizers and Federal troops passing through on their way to Washington, D.C. Many felt these riots would be the catalyst that would pull Maryland out of the Union and into the Confederacy.[2] On April 20, President Lincoln sent a message to both Governor Hicks and Baltimore's Mayor Brown asking them to come to Washington to discuss the situation in Maryland. Lincoln hoped to preserve the peace there. Maryland requested that no more troops be sent through Baltimore and said that the incidents of the previous day were a result of Baltimore's desire to protect itself. Hicks and Brown went on to explain that the destruction of the railroad bridges north of Baltimore was designed to prevent bloodshed and was not an act of hostility toward the government. They also told the president that his call for seventy-five thousand troops was viewed by Marylanders as an act of war against the South and a violation of its constitutional rights. Therefore, it should have surprised no one that the people would resent the passage of Northern troops through the city of Baltimore heading south. The troops that were at that moment nearing Baltimore were turned back toward Harrisburg, Pennsylvania, thus preventing further violence and bloodshed in Baltimore.

At this time, the Maryland legislature met only in even years, so it was not scheduled to be in session in 1861. Governor Hicks was being urged to call a special session that Henry Winter Davis, a member of the Know-Nothing Party and a serving member of the United States Congress, was convinced

Riots broke out in Baltimore on April 19, 1861, when Federal troops attempted to march through the city. *Library of Congress.*

would lead to secession for Maryland and civil war. It was his opinion that if the legislature could be kept from sitting, the Union would remain intact.[3] In a speech before Congress, Davis asked whether Marylanders really wanted to "break up and destroy the Constitution which Washington founded," stating that "peaceful secession is a delusion."[4]

Commissioners from the states of Alabama and Mississippi wrote to Governor Hicks and other leaders in an effort to persuade them to join their cause. Governor Hicks, who was opposed to secession in general, continued to assert Maryland's neutrality, both for the state's protection and so that the people could help mediate the conflict between the hostile sides. An editorial in the *Frederick Herald* advocated neutrality for Maryland, stating that the election of Abraham Lincoln as president was not sufficient cause to secede but that coercion should not be used to keep the Southern states from seceding.[5]

Others were ready to choose sides. One was Thomas Gough of St. Mary's County, who in a speech at a celebration of Washington's birthday said, "The States of Virginia and Maryland having grown together in prosperity, they should cling together in adversity. Like the Siamese Twins to divide them would be to kill them both."[6] On April 23, the largest public meeting ever held in St. Mary's County took place at Leonardtown, when both military and civilian men met to consider the present crisis and adopt measures for the defense and security of their rights and their homes. Among the resolutions adopted was to pledge their sympathies "earnestly and devotedly" with the cause and people of the seceded states and to oblige themselves to aid by every means in their power in securing the independence of those states and any others as may choose to join them. They also imposed a local tax on the citizens of the county in order to raise $10,000 ($357,700 in 2024 dollars) for the purpose of purchasing arms and ammunitions for the citizens so that they may defend their rights and the honor and interest of the state. The women, on that same day, presented a Confederate flag to Captain Riley and his Riley's Rifles before they marched off to Richmond.

Governor Hicks was finally convinced to convene a special Secession Convention in late April, after the upheaval in Baltimore. President Lincoln knew the legislature was about to meet and instructed General Winfield Scott not to interfere with the lawmakers. It was assumed that they would take action to arm the people against the Union, but Lincoln did not feel that arrest or dispersion of the members would be justifiable. They had the legal right to assemble, and if arrested or dispersed, they could not be held long and would simply reconvene as soon as possible. Instead, he instructed Scott to wait for the outcome and act accordingly. He said that if they decided to arm the people of Maryland against the United States, Scott was to "adopt the most prompt and efficient means to counteract, even, if necessary, to the bombardment of their cities."[7]

The General Assembly normally met in the state capital of Annapolis, but it and Baltimore had been put under Federal military control as a result of the riots, so they planned to meet in Frederick, Maryland. Governor Hicks continued to promote neutrality, saying that Maryland should not take sides against the Federal government until it had committed outrages against the people of the state. He hoped that by staying neutral, the warring sides would be forced to "transfer the field of battle from our soil, so that our lives and property may be secure."[8]

The assembly voted 53–13 against secession on April 29, not because they did not sympathize with the South but because they felt they did not have the constitutional right to leave the Union. Many felt that the vote should have been put to the people of Maryland in a referendum and that the outcome would have thus been different.

Despite the vote against secession, the assembly did vote in favor of two additional measures, showing that their support for the Union went only so far. These measures kept the railroad lines to the north closed and called

Secretary of War Simon Cameron prevented the Maryland General Assembly from meeting in September 1861 by arresting many of its members. *Library of Congress.*

for President Lincoln to remove the Federal troops from the state—but the troops stayed until 1865.

The Maryland Assembly tried to meet again, in September, but Simon Cameron, secretary of war, did not allow it. He said, "The passage of any act of secession by the legislature of Maryland must be prevented. If necessary, all or any part of the members must be arrested." One-third of the legislators were arrested and taken to Fort McHenry, which prevented a new vote and brought the special session to an end before it even began.

The postmaster general, Montgomery Blair, had a notice published in the *St. Mary's Beacon* on August 30 announcing President Lincoln's "interdicting commercial intercourse with the so-called Confederate States," which was to include written correspondence. As in so many things, the people of Southern Maryland simply ignored the order.[9] So, Lafayette Baker, chief of the U.S. Federal Detective Police, came to Southern Maryland in October 1861, intent on shutting down the mail service to the South.[10] Secretary of War Cameron sent three companies of one hundred men each from General Joseph Hooker's Third Indiana Cavalry to accompany Baker and, if necessary, permanently occupy the area.[11] They did stay and took up headquarters near Budd's Ferry, with another force in Port Tobacco and a third in Leonardtown.

Baker said that "the result of every Cabinet meeting at Washington was reported in Richmond within twenty-four hours after it was held. The secret was that every postmaster in Lower Maryland…with three exceptions, were disloyal."[12] His first target was the Great Mills Post Office, which was apparently a repository for mail heading into and out of the Confederacy. The postmaster, John S. Travis, was arrested and brought to Washington, D.C., charged with carrying the mails to and from Maryland into Virginia. The provost marshal of Baltimore provided an abundance of proof against Travis and others. Baker also recommended closing the post office at Newport, which was very close to Allen's Fresh and being run by a "first-class rebel." Rather than close any other offices, Baker compiled a list of loyal citizens who were willing to accept appointments to the position of postmaster, saying that it would be a great inconvenience to the few loyal people residing in Southern Maryland to shut all of the post offices. Other arrests were made, as it was not just the postmasters carrying the letters.

One loyal citizen on Baker's list was John R. Biscoe of Great Mills, Maryland. He sent a letter to Secretary of War Simon Cameron on November 18, 1861, in the name of all the Union men of St. Mary's County. In it, he named a number of Rebels who were doing all in their power to aid the Rebel army and who had used most treasonable language toward the government. He was asking for these men to be arrested and "taken out of our midst," as the Rebel numbers were growing every day and the loyal citizens no longer felt safe in their own homes.[13]

To combat this illicit trade and to "interrupt the enemy's communications; drive from those waters every hostile bottom; and protect loyal citizens," Union Naval Commander James H. Ward proposed a flotilla in April 1861, with a view to service in the Chesapeake and its tributaries—chiefly the Potomac River. The Potomac Flotilla was formed and arrived in the Potomac River on May 1, 1861. Its main purposes were to restrict communication between Maryland and Virginia; limit Confederate activity along the river, both on it and on shore; and defend Washington, D.C. It was based out of the Washington Navy Yard but also had a coaling station at the Wicomico River and Piney Point, both in St. Mary's County, Maryland.

Yet the nightly smuggling of supplies to Virginia continued. Potomac Flotilla commander Thomas T. Craven[14] wrote on August 11, 1861: "From all I can see and learn of the people of Maryland I am convinced that along the shores of the Potomac there is not one in twenty who is true to the

The following order has just been published by the Postmaster General:

POST OFFICE DEPARTMENT, Aug. 24, 1861.

The President of the United States directs, that his proclamation of the 16th inst., interdicting commercial intercourse with the so called Confederate States, shall be applied to correspondence with those States, and has devolved upon this department the enforcement of so much of its interdict as relates to such correspondence.

The officers and agent of this Department will, therefore, without further instructions, lose no time in putting an end to written intercourse with these States by causing the arrest of any Express Agent or other persons who shall after the promulgation of this order, receive letters to be carried to or from these States, and will seize all such letters and forward them to this Department.

(Signed) M. BLAIR,
Postmaster General.

St. Mary's Beacon, August 30, 1861.

Union, and I sometimes think there are many hundreds of them thoroughly organized into companies, perhaps regiments, and prepared to act against the Government at any moment." No one could come and go on the Potomac River without the Confederacy knowing about it. There were signal agents working on both sides of the river, forwarding intelligence to Southern leaders. This allowed the smugglers to continue their work without being molested or stopped.

Maryland's Governor Hicks wrote to Andrew Harwood, commander of the Washington Navy Yard, "that an extensive carrying of clothing, provisions, etc. is going on upon and across the lower Potomac." A note intercepted by one of the flotilla vessels from Confederate President Jefferson Davis included a line about all the citizens of both Charles and St. Mary's Counties, Maryland being friends of the South.

The batteries that had appeared on the Virginia shore of the Potomac River after the Battle of Manassas were harassing the Federal vessels as they tried to navigate the river to and from Washington. By October 1861, the Confederates controlled fifteen miles of the river, which brought shipping to a standstill. In November, General George McClellan sent twelve thousand troops under General Hooker to Budd's Ferry, in Charles County, Maryland, to build Union batteries on that shore to try to roust the troops from the opposite shore. The United States Navy declared the river closed, out of concern for the safety of their ships, not due to the effectiveness of the shore batteries. This was an embarrassment for the North, as the Union capital was now besieged and blockaded, and a victory for the morale of the Confederacy. All supplies and men now had to be diverted to Baltimore and transported overland from there to Washington, D.C., and the citizens of St. Mary's County were greatly inconvenienced, as all steamboat operations between Washington and Baltimore had been interrupted "to their great injury and detriment."[15]

On March 8, 1862, President Lincoln issued General Order No. 3 ordering that the army and navy cooperate in an effort to capture the enemy batteries on the Potomac and clear the river for navigation. The Potomac Flotilla removed the Confederate batteries, and the river reopened shortly thereafter. The fifteen miles that had been closed to Union traffic for five months were now reopened as formerly, as the lifeline in and out of Washington, D.C. However, navigation on the river remained a periodic problem throughout the entire war.

In April 1862, General Benjamin Butler arrived in Maryland and declared martial law. He was able to restore the Baltimore and Ohio (B&O) Railroad

General Benjamin Butler declared martial law in Maryland in April 1862 and stationed troops throughout the entire state. *Library of Congress.*

line between Annapolis and Washington, D.C., which now allowed troop transports to bypass the Potomac, "where Confederates were causing trouble." His troops were already occupying the Naval Academy in Annapolis, and he was told to occupy Baltimore as well, in order to protect all transport links, rail, sea and land. He accomplished this by May 13. Butler also positioned Union troops throughout the rest of the state, including Leonardtown in Southern Maryland, which became the headquarters for a mounted cavalry unit. A curfew was imposed on the residents of Chaptico, also in St. Mary's County, in May 1862, which required that all lights be put out and business be suspended by 9:30 p.m. under penalty of arrest.

Arrests of Confederate sympathizers and critics of both President Lincoln and the United States government soon followed. Those arrested in Baltimore included militia Captain John Merryman, who was held without trial in defiance of a writ of habeas corpus, which led to the Supreme Court case *Ex Parte Merryman*. Chief Justice, and Marylander, Roger B. Taney ruled that the arrest of Merryman was unconstitutional without congressional authorization, but President Lincoln simply ignored the ruling. Others arrested across the state included newspaper owners and editors, and nine of the newspapers were shut down by the federal government, including all of those in Southern Maryland.

Before it could be silenced completely, the Baltimore-based newspaper *South* reported that Annapolis, the state capital, had been seized and converted into a military depot; the railroads had been seized and converted into military roads; and the steamboats had been seized and converted into military transports. The Federal troops had established a military despotism over the state and all its population.

Still, none of this quelled the zealousness of the Confederate sympathizers in Southern Maryland. The people paid little attention, life went on as usual and their dealings with Virginia continued—albeit more cautiously. Their once-open exchange of goods and information continued as always, but now in secret.

One of those who was "true to the Union" was William J. Blackistone, who was appointed as the draft commissioner for St. Mary's County. He wrote to Maryland's newly elected governor, Augustus Bradford, in 1862 that "there is not a Union man that I recognize within seven miles of my residence." When Blackistone sent the enrollment books to Annapolis in October, he listed 1,652 men of draft age, 47 of whom were dismissed by medical officer Dr. James H. Miles of Chaptico as physically unfit for service. Another 120 had either joined the Confederate forces or were incarcerated at the Old Capital Prison in Washington, D.C., for showing Southern sympathies. That left 1,485 for service in the Union army.

According to Commander Andrew A. Harwood[16] of the Potomac Flotilla, pungies and other small vessels rowed by African Americans regularly crossed the river carrying supplies. He assumed these men were forced into this service by their masters, who thus remained out of harm's way. But in at least one instance, arrests were made of both white and Black men. On August 11, a report was sent to the navy yard that the USS *Freeborn*, of the flotilla, had arrested sixteen white and nine Black men on the Potomac for "engaging in improper communication and traffic between Maryland and Virginia. With these parties [were] seized a quantity of stores."[17] Among the supplies being carried was salt, which sold for 100 Maryland (not Confederate) dollars in Virginia. Whiskey also was transported and sold for 10 Maryland dollars a gallon—along with bacon, coffee, sugar, newspapers, the mail and men. Corn and wheat were brought back. The principal depots were identified as Leonardtown and Wicomico Bay on the Maryland shore and the Nomini River, Pope's Bridge and Machodoc Creek on the Virginia side.

Commander Harwood also reported that same fall that the merchants in Leonardtown had laid in five times the usual stores of goods for the winter. These were goods that they refused to sell to the local people, except by wholesale and at exorbitant prices. One man in particular, a Mr. Colton, who lived in the vicinity of Blackistone Island, was under suspicion for a number of reasons. He claimed to be a Union man but had refused an officer's appointment so was not serving. He was very outspoken and often betrayed Southern sympathies. He openly spoke of wanting salt, but it was known that there were three or four sacks already in his barn. He also made it known that he had a spyglass through which he could see fifteen miles up and down the river and that his boats could make the Potomac crossing in forty minutes. In spite of all this open talk, the flotilla officers could not catch him performing a single illegal act. Nor were they ever able to arrest Leonardtown merchant Mr. Plunkett, who they knew had boats that he used to convey news and Rebels from Maryland to Virginia.

In October 1862, Commander Harwood sent a report to Secretary of the Navy Gideon Welles requesting that a cavalry force be sent to the principal trading towns of Leonardtown, Chaptico, Great Mills and Millstone Landing (now part of Lexington Park), all in St. Mary's County, Maryland, and Port Tobacco in Charles County, to assist in curbing the illicit trading between Maryland and Virginia. The flotilla was doing its part, stopping and seizing vessels on the rivers, but they had no arresting authority on land so needed the assistance of land forces to prevent the stockpiling of goods and to watch the activity of the known sympathizers.

By 1864, the Potomac River had been laid out in divisions, with vessels assigned to each area. They were to cruise their sections from dusk until dawn and lay at anchor during the day but never in the same place two days in a row. No bells were to be struck at night, and on foggy or misty nights, the guard was to be doubled. A naval force was always kept close to

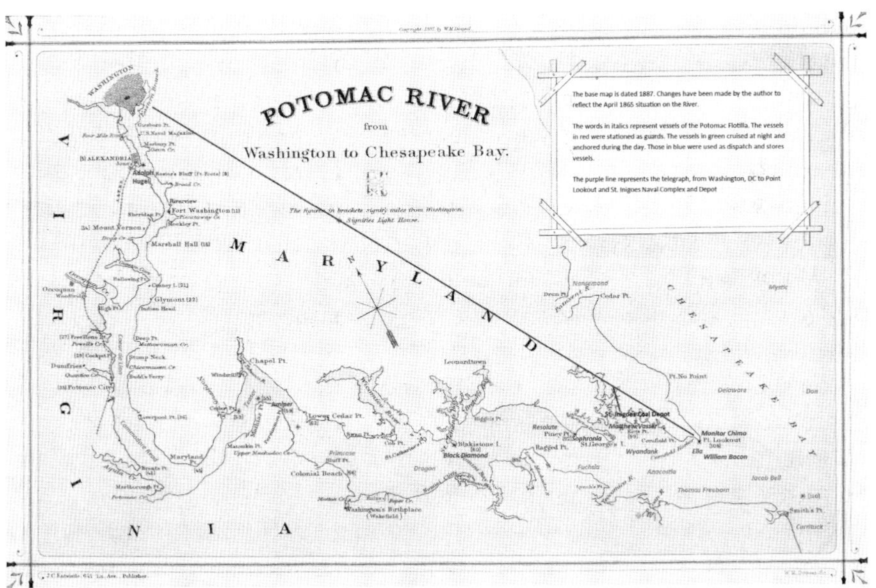

By 1864, flotilla Commander Parker had the Potomac River laid out in divisions, with vessels assigned to each area. They were to cruise their sections from dusk until dawn and lay at anchor during the day. Some stayed in place to guard shore stations, and others traveled as supply and dispatch vessels. *By the author.*

Point Lookout, which since the summer of 1863 had been designated as a prisoner-of-war camp. The flotilla officer in command of that division was to be in constant communication with the senior army officer there—the only land forces that had been sent to St. Mary's County in spite of the flotilla commanders' continued requests. The commander even offered to allow them tenting grounds at one of the flotilla's coaling depots. Guard ships were also stationed at Alexandria, the coal depot at St. Inigoes, Piney Point Lighthouse and Blackistone Island. One vessel was kept at the ready to serve as a dispatch and supply boat, and others were used as convoy support for troop transports.

With all of the unrest and illicit activity going on in Southern Maryland, it was only natural that when John Wilkes Booth assassinated President Lincoln on April 14, 1865, the manhunt focused on that region and the government called on the Potomac Flotilla for aid. Secretary of War Edwin Stanton issued the following War Department Bulletin, which was printed in the *St. Mary's Gazette* on April 27:

> *THE ASSASSINATION*
> *The Accomplices in Maryland—the Disloyalists to be punished—War Department Washington. April 22, 1865.—Major General Dix. New York:—The counties of Prince George's, Charles and St. Mary's, have, during the whole war, been noted for hostility to the government and their protection to rebel blockade-runners, rebel spies, and every species of public enemy. The murderers of the President harbored there before the murder, and Booth fled in that direction. If he escapes, it will be owing to rebel accomplices in that region. The military commander of the department will speedily take measures to bring these rebel sympathizers and accomplices in the murder to a sense of their criminal conduct.*

Acting Master of the USS *Delaware* J.H. Eldridge sent a letter to Acting Master of *Thomas Freeborn* W.A. Arthur, both of the Potomac Flotilla, stating:

> *In consequence of information having been received that the murderer of the President has been seen in this vicinity, I would request that you patrol the bay from Point Lookout to the mouth* [of] *Patuxent River, keeping a strict watch on the movements of all vessels and on any small boats that may attempt to leave the west shore of the bay. All steamers bound down the bay you will hail and order them to proceed to Point Lookout and remain until further orders.*

Edwin Stanton, the secretary of war, then sent a notice to Major James R. O'Beirne.[18] He was relieved from his regular duties and was to direct all of his attention to the capture and arrest of the murderer of the president and the assassins who attempted to murder Secretary Seward. So, with his detective force, O'Beirne pushed to Leonardtown and searched the entire area looking for Booth and Herold. Preparations were then made to search Allen's Fresh, and a second force started from Point Lookout, sweeping the peninsula up to Medley's Neck. A third force headed toward Chappell's Point.

The entire peninsula was searched, with the forces marching in close skirmish line across it, but they found nothing of note. On April 19, Lieutenant Luther Baker, Lafayette Baker's cousin, sent six of his men to the area, but they, too, returned emptyhanded. A call went out to increase the strength of the Potomac Flotilla, hoping to create such a dense picket line that no boat would be able to get through. One of the vessels assigned to join them was the *Black Diamond*, one of over six hundred ships chartered by the Quartermaster Department to transport supplies to the army. Stationed mostly at the Alexandria Quartermaster Depot, *Black Diamond* was immediately available so was sent to join this special force, not knowing that it was too late or that this would be its final mission.

CHAPTER 2

THE LIGHTS ARE NOT SAFE!

Navigation is now more dangerous on the two rivers. Most of the buoys have been taken up and the light boats burnt. The light houses remain.
—Alexandria Gazette, *May 13, 1861*

At the start of the Civil War, there were six navigational aids of various types on the Potomac River between Alexandria, Virginia, and Piney Point, Maryland.

Piney Point Lighthouse, built in 1836, was the first lighthouse erected on the Potomac River. A light vessel had been stationed in the area since 1821 to mark hazardous shoals at Piney Point on the Maryland side and at Ragged Point on the opposite shore. Piney Point's original lighting apparatus was visible for ten miles. That system of ten oil lamps and reflectors was replaced by a more efficient fifth-order Fresnel lens in 1855, which increased the visibility to eleven miles. A coal depot for the Potomac Flotilla was established at Piney Point, but delivery and compliance issues arose, so it was relocated to Cross Manor, in St. Inigoes.

A second light vessel was authorized in 1821, for Upper Cedar Point, on the southerly side of the channel off the mouth of the Tobacco River, in the area of the river referred to as "the narrows." Congress authorized the stationing of an additional light vessel in the narrows, off Lower Cedar Point below Kettle Bottom, in 1825. It was moored on the west side of the channel.

In 1861, the two lightships at Cedar Point were burned by Rebels from Virginia and Maryland, led by John Goldsmith. A report of activities sent from the Potomac Flotilla vessel *Rescue* on September 30, 1861, lists the names of the men who burned them. The list included men who lived on both the Maryland and Virginia sides of the Potomac: Jonathon Johnson, William Campbell, Frank Clements, Alexander Campbell and Alfred Aubey. In addition to burning the ships, they also carried goods from Maryland to Virginia, and it was while rowing across with a fully laden vessel that they were captured.[19] Both stations remained vacant until 1864, when new vessels were finally put in place. The newspaper reported, "Navigation is now more dangerous on the two rivers. Most of the buoys have been taken up and the light boats burnt. The light houses remain. Volunteer companies are forming all through the Northern Neck of Virginia. The militia are also drilling with determined activity. But how utterly exposed is the dear and unoffending people."[20]

At this same time, the Confederates were also methodically destroying the buoys and channel markers on the Potomac. One schooner, *Christina*, had already run aground while trying to navigate the river at night. In his report to Gideon Welles, secretary of the navy, in April 1861, Washington Commandant John Dahlgren stated that the river pilots were concerned about the difficulty in navigating the Kettle Bottom shoals without the channel markers and asked that the buoys be replaced. Secretary Welles suggested that one of the river steamers, with one or more pilots, should be sent down from Washington to replace the buoys immediately.[21] By June, this had not been done, and on the fourteenth of the month, the schooner *Christiana Keen*, which had been running at night, found itself outside the channel, unable to navigate this intricate section of the river. It ran aground just opposite Cedar Point, "not far from where the light-boat was, where also a buoy was until two or three days ago." It was burned by a party of thirty Virginians who put out of Chotank Creek, intent on its destruction, in rowboats with their oar locks muffled for silent rowing. Because the Piney Point and Blackistone Island lights were burning, the master of the *Christiana Keen* had erroneously assumed that all the others on the Potomac River were as well, including the lightships on the flats where he grounded.[22]

As a rule, vessels were not permitted to sail at night, and it was recommended by the officers of the Potomac Flotilla that they anchor overnight at St. Mary's River, Blackistone Lighthouse, Nanjemoy or Aquia, each of which had a government guard vessel in the area to offer protection from Rebels. In the absence of buoys, lightboats and other marks, navigation between Cedar and Maryland Points was simply too hazardous for the night. Some buoys remained, but there was no guarantee that they were in their proper position or that they would not be removed at any moment by Confederate forces. It was also recommended that vessels always sail in pairs and that those trading on the Potomac be armed with muskets to further protect themselves.

Permission was also given "to procure, equip and station in the Potomac River such number of small vessels as may be found necessary to its safe navigation,"[23] but this took time. Finally, on October 24, 1862, Rear Admiral William B. Shubrick, chairman of the Lighthouse Board, reported that a forty-four-foot-long spar buoy had been placed off Cobbs Point, at Kettle Bottom.[24]

Two lighthouses farther down the Potomac, in St. Mary's County, Maryland, were also threatened, but neither was destroyed. On December 11, 1861, Captain Shore of the steamer *Chamberlin* disembarked when he saw a distress flag flying from the Piney Point Lighthouse. Inside the lighthouse, the wife of Keeper Robert J. Marshall reported that "five or six loads of rebels crossed the river every night into Virginia with provisions etc.; [and] that there was $10,000 [$357,700 in 2024 dollars] worth of goods, ammunition, clothing, etc., in the woods just above the lighthouse to be carried over. Men came to her every day and asked her if any of the U.S. cutters were about and told her she had better keep away as they intended to destroy the lighthouse."[25] Piney Point became a coal depot for the Potomac Flotilla in September 1862, but after two years, it was moved to a more suitable location on the St. Mary's River at St. Inigoes.

Three years later, in May 1864, a group of Confederates attacked the Blackistone Lighthouse on Blackistone Island,[26] destroying the lens and lamp and carrying off fifteen gallons of oil. Keeper Jerome McWilliams was well acquainted with the lead perpetrator, John Goldsmith,[27] so was able to convince him, man to man, friend to friend, not to burn down the structure.[28]

An official report of the raid was submitted by Foxhall A. Parker, commander of the Potomac Flotilla, on May 21, to Gideon Welles from on board the USS *King Philip*, St. Mary's, Maryland. In it, he said:

> *Sir, I have to report to the Department that on the night of the 19th instant 12 rebels, headed by a man named Goldsmith, landed in a small boat at Blakistone* [sic] *Island, and destroyed the lens and lamp and carried off 15 gallons of oil belonging to the lighthouse at that point, without doing further injury. I have requested Colonel Draper, commanding at Point Lookout, to station a guard at Blakistone Island, at Piney Point, and on board the light-ship off Smith's Point, during the time that the vessels of*

Left: Rear Admiral William B. Shubrick served as the chairman of the Lighthouse Board, which fell under the Department of the Treasury, and was responsible for the construction and maintenance of all lighthouses and other aids to navigation. *National Archives and Records Administration.*

Below: Piney Point Lighthouse was the first lighthouse to be built on the Potomac River. Both the keeper's wife and the structure itself were threatened by Confederate raiders on a regular basis. It later served as a coal depot for the Potomac Flotilla. *St. Mary's County Museum Division.*

> *the Potomac Flotilla are required for the protection of the army transports at Aquia Creek, Belle Plain, and in the Rappahannock and for the convoying of vessels carrying prisoners of war to Fort Delaware and Point Lookout. And I am of the opinion that while there are so many rebel sympathizers in Maryland and on the eastern shore of Virginia none of the lighthouses there located are safe without a guard on shore to protect them. I have the honor to be etc.*

Colonel A.G. Draper, commander of the District of Southern Maryland, replied to Parker from his headquarters at Point Lookout, stating that he had dispatched a sergeant and twenty-two men to Piney Point and was sending a lieutenant to consult with Parker about the situation at Blackistone Island. He went on to say that the cavalry detachment in Leonardtown could not be spared at that time.

While waiting for replacement equipment, Keeper McWilliams used a handheld lamp to light the tower each night. The new lantern and lens were installed that July.

Keeper McWilliams's problems began in June 1861, when he was threatened the first time. During a routine examination of the Potomac River, the USS *Resolute* of the Potomac Flotilla landed at Blackistone Island and learned from the keeper that he had recently received a letter threatening him with violence and the building with destruction, if the light was not extinguished at once. McWilliams did not comply, instead requesting arms and ammunition from the flotilla so that he could defend both himself and the property. The perpetrators were identified by the flotilla commander as a Virginian named Blackwell and two men named Rey and Haresiding, of Breton's Bay, Maryland, but they never acted on their threats so were not arrested.[29]

The following year, a complaint was filed against Keeper McWilliams by a master pilot named Robert Watter because the light was not lit. E.R. McCrea, then commander of the Potomac Flotilla, also reported that it was dark at this time. The excuse given by McWilliams was that his oil had been used up by the vessels in the flotilla, so he did not have any to use in the lantern. In February 1862, Keeper McWilliams did begin sending receipts showing that the flotilla had been using his oil. Supply depots for the flotilla were eventually established at Piney Point Lighthouse and elsewhere for coal, oil and other supplies, which reduced expenses for the flotilla and left lighthouse supplies intact.

Copy

Navy Department.
Washington May 27th 1864.

Sir.

I have the honor to enclose herewith, a Copy of a Communication dated the 21st inst, received from Commander F. A. Parker, commanding Potomac Flotilla, in relation to the recent rebel raid upon Blakistones Island, in which he expresses the opinion, that the Light-Houses in Maryland and on the Eastern Shore of Virginia are not safe without a guard on Shore to protect them.

Very Respect.y &c

Hon: S. P. Chase (Signed) Gideon Welles.
Secy of Treasury. Secy of Navy.

AL

Gideon Welles, the secretary of the navy, sent a letter to Salmon P. Chase, secretary of the treasury, informing him of the raid on the Blackistone Lighthouse and expressing the need for a guard on shore to protect them. *National Archives and Records Administration.*

Lighthouse Keeper Jerome McWilliams was written up on a number of occasions for not having the lantern properly lit. *St. Mary's County Museum Division.*

Throughout the war, many vessels were stopped while passing in the vicinity of Blackistone Island and taken by the Potomac Flotilla for lack of passes, improper paperwork, questionable cargo and so on. In May 1863, the flotilla vessel *Eureka* was stationed off the island, and in June, someone from the island hailed it and a small boat was sent ashore in response. The officer in charge captured seven men who were crossing from Virginia as refugees, with one being kept as a prisoner of war.

An official notice to mariners was published in the newspaper in December 1864 and was met with great consternation. It stated that in view of the danger caused by ice, the Lighthouse Board was ordering the immediate removal of the two light vessels at Upper and Lower Cedar Point to Alexandria, Virginia, for the winter. It went on to say that no lights would be shown until further notice from either of those stations. These two new vessels had just been placed at these stations on August 31, 1864. As recommended, the

U.S. Army was providing each of these vessels a competent guard for their protection, to prevent any further incidents with Rebel forces.

The Lighthouse Board had reason to be concerned about the ice, based on the conditions of previous winters, going back as far as 1852. The Potomac Flotilla began reporting problems with ice in January 1864. Flotilla Commander Parker sent a telegram to Secretary of the Navy Welles about the ice situation on the seventh. In it, he said, "The river is frozen across (so I am informed) to Maryland Point from Mt. Vernon—3 schooners 'fast in the ice.' Flotilla cannot afford them aid; suggest that military authorities be apprised and take such measures for their relief and <u>protection against guerillas</u> as they may deem advisable."[30] The problem with ice on the Potomac was reported in a letter that same day to R.F. Loper, the owner of *Black Diamond*, which was under contract to the Federal government. In it, the writer stated that the vessels recently placed by Loper under charter to the Quartermaster Department had been certified and were ready; however, they were unable to get out of Alexandria "in consequence of ice." He went on to say that ice was lodged against the bridge in Washington and packed to depths of ten feet, keeping those vessels in port as well. In closing, he wrote that the weather was currently clear and cold, but he was apprehensive of an

The Potomac River often froze over, causing transportation issues, and this put the lightships in danger of attack by Confederate raiders. *Maryland State Archives.*

LOCAL NEWS.

RIVER NEWS.—The Potomac is again open but is filled with floating ice, which is blocking up opposite Giesboro. This, it is believed, however, will not very seriously interfere with navigation, as the ice has become softened, and can very easily be cut through.

As to the condition of the lower Potomac nothing is known here, as there has been no arrivals from a point further down than Alexandria.

A fleet of transports, some of which are going to Savannah with Quartermaster's stores, will be despatched from here and Alexandria under convoy of the ice-boat Atlantic. This morning the propeller Black Diamond was engaged in taking on board a large quantity of Adams' Express freight which has accumulated here since the Ice blockade, and will sail this evening for City Point.

Up to 9 o'clock this morning the Alexandria and Washington ferry boats had not resumed their trips, but it was expected that they would do so in the course of the day.

Washington, D.C. Evening Star, February 1, 1865.

extended, cold winter. Three days later, Loper received a letter from Jacob Bush, a colleague in Delaware City, Delaware, in which Bush wrote that the canal there was frozen up tight, so no boats were moving along it at the present time. He said it had been that way for the past week and noted that he had heard that the Potomac was "frozen tight" as well.

In response to this Notice to Mariners, a letter was immediately sent from Rufus Ingalls, quartermaster general for the Army of the Potomac, to General Montgomery Meigs, quartermaster general of the army, who then forwarded it with additional comments to the secretary of war, pointing out that the risk of loss by damage from ice to the light vessels was much less important than the sure loss of transport vessels if the lights were removed. One of these transport vessels was the *Massachusetts*, which had been under contract to the Quartermaster Department since the fall of 1863. The letter also pointed out that the last time the light vessels were pulled, the Quartermaster Department stationed vessels of its own as temporary light boats at those spots. That was necessary after the vessel *Louise* ran aground, having failed to negotiate the channel in the absence of the lights. As a way of softening the request, the letter offered all possible

Foxhall Parker served as the executive officer of the Washington Navy Yard in 1861–62, became a commander in July 1862 and then took command of the Potomac Flotilla in 1863. He was its final commander, serving until July 1865. *Naval History Command.*

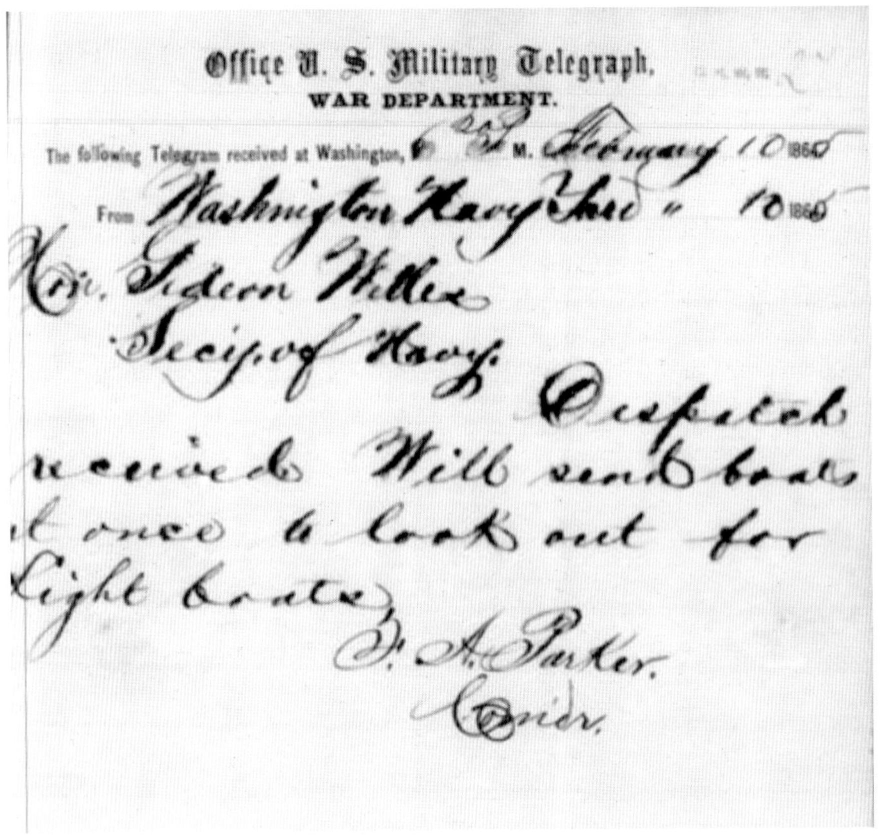

Office U. S. Military Telegraph.
WAR DEPARTMENT.

The following Telegram received at Washington, 6 30 P.M. February 10 1865

From Washington Navy Yard 10 1865

Hon. Gideon Welles
Secy. of Navy.
Dispatch received. Will send boats at once to look out for Light boats.
F. A. Parker.
Comdr.

Commander Foxhall Parker was ordered to send vessels from the Potomac Flotilla to guard the light boats at Upper and Lower Cedar Point. *National Archives and Records Administration.*

assistance to the light boats when needed, via the tugs constantly plying the river for the Quartermaster Department. The vessels were soon returned to their stations.

Twice the following winter, in February 1865, the *Washington Evening Star* reported about the ice on the Potomac, writing on the first that the *Black Diamond* was heading to City Point, Virginia, loaded with a large quantity of Adams Express freight, which had accumulated since the ice blockade. It went on to say that an iceboat was escorting a fleet of transports down the Potomac as well, since the condition of the lower Potomac was not known. On the twentieth, the paper reported that the river was open but that vessels were having a great deal of difficulty navigating the bend in the river where the ice had lodged. The *Black Diamond* was once again being sent out to City Point, this time with a load of salted pork and beef for the army, and ferryboats were running again, but not on their usual schedules due to the large quantities of ice blocking the mouths of the channel in areas. And Commander Parker was again ordered to send boats from the Potomac Flotilla to look after the light boats and keep them safe.

Other vessels had refused to travel at night, unless under special orders, for fear of running aground, which was causing delays in the transport of goods and troops. Captain James G.C. Lee, assistant quartermaster, Alexandria Depot, requested additional iceboats for use on the Potomac at this same time, noting that there was likely to be at least another month of interruptions due to ice. With the arrival of spring and the eventual return of the lightships and buoys, navigation on the river returned to normal.

CHAPTER 3

THE VESSELS

In the spring of 1865, there were a total of 612 vessels being chartered by the Quartermaster Department.
—Report of the Quartermaster General to the Secretary of War for the year ending June 30, 1865

During the nineteenth century, the Quartermaster Department was not yet a specialized military unit with its own transport vehicles or vessels. Instead, the department relied on contracted workers and also detailed soldiers to work onboard vessels hired or commandeered for transporting troops and supplies. When the United States capital was in danger and the railroads continued to be obstructed, no mode of transporting troops and goods existed except on the water. J. Edgar Thomson of the War Department stepped in and arranged for ships to be placed into service by whatever means available.

On April 19, 1861, two days after Virginia voted to secede from the Union, President Lincoln confiscated four steamboats belonging to the Potomac Steamboat Company, which was part of the Richmond, Fredericksburg and Potomac Railroad system. At least three of these were put into the service of the Federal government.

That same day, Thomson contacted Captain Richard F. Loper, asking for his help in obtaining boats for the transporting of troops destined for Washington, D.C. Loper was a shipper in Philadelphia, Pennsylvania. He had been in the business of building, navigating and freighting vessels

The Quartermaster Depot at Alexandria, Virginia, served as the home base for many of the vessels being used as troop transports, including the *Massachusetts*. *Library of Congress*.

and steamboats for over forty years, having first supplied vessels to the government during the Mexican-American War, so he was known to the War Department. He was a pioneer of contract shipbuilding and an inventor of innovative screw propellers for ships. He also invented the composite hull—an iron frame overlaid with wood planking (used on the *Black Diamond*)—a compound marine engine and a return tubular boiler. He obtained three patents related to propellers in 1844 and 1845.

Loper was instrumental in designing some of the government's ships during the Civil War, using his new propeller and composite-style hull, with the help of R.B. Forbes. When the war began, Loper was listed as a shipper in the Philadelphia Business Directories, but by 1861, he was listed as the president of the Philadelphia Steam Propeller Company. Both entries have the same address listed as his place of business: 224 South Delaware Avenue.

For most of April 1861 Loper spent his time finding and chartering vessels for the Quartermaster Department, eventually including one of his own, the *Black Diamond*. By the end of the war, there were 612 vessels under contract to the U.S. Quartermaster Department. Under the system in use at that time, the Quartermaster Department paid the owners of private vessels chartered for government use. The owners were then responsible for paying the captains and crews. This eliminated pension and claim rights for these civilian employees and their families. The enlisted men working on the vessels and the soldiers being transported on the *Massachusetts* were not affected by this policy, so some of their families did make successful claims to collect them. It was also the owner's responsibility to keep the vessel in good repair and to outfit it with the supplies needed for service. The pilotage and port fees were paid by the government.

These ships' contracts all stated that "war risk" was to be borne by the United States and that "marine risk" was to be borne by the owners. If a vessel was damaged by enemy shelling or was captured, the government would pay. But if the damage was the result of a storm, pilot error or collision with another vessel that was not an intentional act by the enemy, the responsibility was the owner's. This was a standard clause in all contracts for vessels hired to serve in the war effort in the Quartermaster Department.

When carrying nothing but government stores and traveling the Potomac River, these vessels carried certificates from Chief Quartermaster D.H. Baker or Assistant Quartermaster Captain Allen, Washington D.C., allowing them to pass through the Potomac Flotilla without being searched.

Each vessel traveling the waters of Maryland—including the Potomac River—was required by law to have a duly trained and certified pilot on board. It was up to the pilot to ensure safe passage to vessels entering the Chesapeake Bay and traveling up and down its tributaries in and out of port. The Association of Maryland Pilots was formed in 1852, although pilots had been in use in the Chesapeake Bay region since the 1640s. In an 1851 opinion, the United States Supreme Court summarized the pilot's job, saying that the pilot is the temporary master charged with the safety of the vessel and cargo and of the lives of those on board. This applied to the charter vessels as well as the vessels of the Potomac Flotilla. Pilots assigned to ships of the flotilla were employed by the commodore commanding, not the vessel's commanding officer. They were paid $65 ($2,325.05 in 2024 dollars) per month plus one ration a day and served as civilians, not members of the military.

THE *BLACK DIAMOND*

The *Black Diamond* was an iron-hulled, wood-planked, second-class steam propeller barge[31] 120 feet long with a 24-foot beam and capable of carrying between 180 and 200 tons of freight. It, along with its three sister ships,[32] was built in 1842 by Hogg & Delamater Iron Works of New York for the Delaware and Raritan Canal Company as a coal transport barge and was owned by R.F. Loper, of Philadelphia. The use of a composite hull was developed and patented by Loper in the 1840s. It was run by a grasshopper-type engine, 18-by-24-inch stroke.

Cornelius DeLamater began his career at the Phoenix Iron Works in New York and took it over when its owner died. DeLamater took charge and formed the new company in partnership with Peter Hogg. The ironworks built steam boilers and machinery as well as vessels and remained in existence until 1857, when Hogg retired. The firm was re-formed as the DeLamater Iron Works and moved from its original location in lower Manhattan to the west side of Manhattan.

Black Diamond was the first of four sister ships designed by John Ericsson and built by Hogg & Delamater to be chartered to the Federal government. The original 1862 contract specified $140 per diem, to be paid to the owner. This rate was reduced to $110 in 1863 and was further reduced to $100 per day in the 1865 contract. During its service, the *Black Diamond* missed time on occasion and was penalized for the days lost. Overall, the Philadelphia

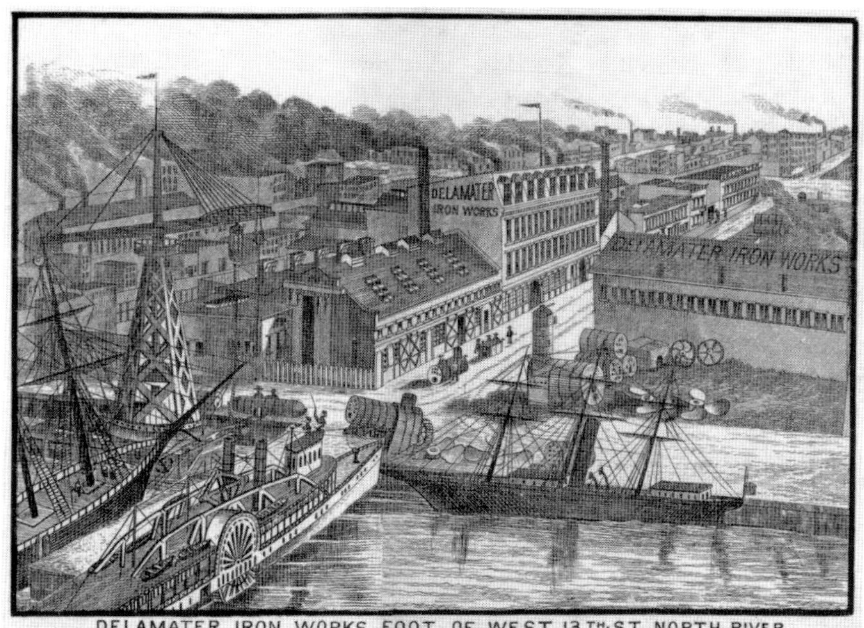

The *Black Diamond* was built in 1842 by Hogg & Delamater Iron Works of New York for use on the Delaware and Raritan Canal as a coal barge. *Wikimedia Commons.*

There are no images of the *Black Diamond*, but it resembled these coal barges, shown at City Point, Virginia. *Library of Congress.*

Steam Propeller Company was paid $30,150[33] for the *Black Diamond*'s time in Federal service. The captain was John Meredith, the engineer was Joseph Husted and the usual crew totaled five. When its daily rate of pay was to be reduced, Loper offered the use of the other vessels along with *Black Diamond* for a lesser fee per vessel but an overall increase in the daily rate for him.

Many repairs and improvements were made to *Black Diamond* by Loper in 1851. These included twin screw propellers of a newly patented design, originally developed by John Ericsson but improved on by Loper.[34] The new propellers were installed on February 28, and two spur mules were added in August.

Black Diamond was chartered by Assistant Quartermaster Captain Boyd and put into the service of the Quartermaster Department in December 1862 by Captain G.H. Orme. This contract ran through September 1863 and was then renewed annually until April 1865. The contract stipulated *Black Diamond* was to be used for the hauling of freight or to be generally available for hire as needed.

Once chartered by the government, the *Black Diamond* continued to serve mostly as a coal transport vessel but now worked the Potomac River

Transportation.—The Washington Star says:—A fleet of transports, some of which are going to Savannah with Quartermasters' stores, will be despatched from Washington and Alexandria under convoy of the ice-boat Atlantic. Yesterday the propeller Black Diamond was engaged in taking on board a large quantity of Adams' Express freight which has accumulated here since the ice blockade, and will sail for City Point.

Arrived.

U. S. steam transport Nightingale, Mannering, Key West 4 ds., with cotton and 18 passengers to U. S. Assistant Quartermaster. She brings 213 bales of cotton consigned to the U. S. Marshal.

U. S. steam transport Fulton, Wotten, Port Royal, S. C., May 30, with mdse. and passengers to U. S. Assistant Quartermaster.

Steamer Neva, Clark, Port Royal, S. C., May 30. Was towed to this port by U. S. steamer Fulton. Came for repairs.

Steamer A. A. Turner, Perkins, Detroit 31 ds., in ballast to master.

Steamer Sea Gull, Kenny, Providence, with mdse. to E. Bynner.

Steamer Walker, Sherin, Philadelphia, with mdse. to J. & N. Briggs.

Steamer Emma Dunn, Burton, Philadelphia, with mdse. to James Hand.

Steamer Black Diamond, Merideth, Philadelphia, with mdse. to Wm. Kirkpatrick & Co.

Steamer Trenton, Wilson, Trenton, N. J., with mdse. to C. J. Hoagland.

Steamer F. W. Brune, Foster, Baltimore, with mdse to Wm. Dalzell.

Ship London, Moore, London and the Isle of Wight May 6, with mdse. and 488 passengers to Grinnell, Minturn & Co. Crossed the Banks of Newfoundland in lat. 44, and saw large quantities of ice, and had dense fogs all the passage.

Top: The Adams Express Company was one of the only companies to hold a Federal contract for mail delivery. *Alexandria Gazette*, February 2, 1865.

Left: The *Black Diamond* often delivered supplies other than coal. *New York Times*, June 3, 1864.

between Alexandria and Washington, D.C., rather than the Delaware and Raritan Canal. It drew less than six feet of water so was ideal for duty on the Potomac and its tributaries. The barge regularly transported coal between Washington and other ports up and down the river, as assigned by the quartermaster, sometimes traveling as far as City Point, Virginia. Other goods it carried included salted pork and beef for the army. It was also sometimes used by the Adams Express Company, which was one of the only companies to hold a Federal contract for the delivery of the United States mail and other packages. And at least once, it received orders to proceed to Baltimore, loaded with army supplies.

The *Massachusetts*

The other vessel in this story is the *Massachusetts*, a 308-ton side-wheel steamer capable of travel in the Chesapeake Bay. It also went by the name *John W.D. Pentz*, which was the name it was registered under as a civilian passenger vessel before the war. It had a single deck, no masts, no gallery, no head and a square stern. The ship was built in New York in 1836 and was originally destined for service on Nantucket but instead operated as a night boat on the Chesapeake and Delaware Canal near Philadelphia. It began working on the Potomac River in the late 1840s and made regular runs from Alexandria to Baltimore, with stops on both sides of the river. The owners were Samuel J. Pentz and John D. Pentz of Baltimore, Maryland; Captain Couch was in charge of the crew; and Joseph White was the master.

The steamer was chartered for service on October 14, 1863, by Captain C.B. Ferguson as a troop transport by Colonel W.L. James, assistant quartermaster, at the rate of $100 ($2,498 in 2024) per diem. The appraised value was $35,000 ($874,300 in 2024), and like the crew on the *Black Diamond*, the men working on it were paid by the owner, not the U.S. government. Based in Alexandria and Washington, D.C., *Massachusetts* made regular runs carrying troops to City Point and Fort Monroe, Virginia.

This is the only known picture of the *Massachusetts*. It was registered as *John W.D. Pentz* before the war while in passenger service. *Maryland Center for History and Culture PP299.964.*

The *Massachusetts* made regular runs carrying troops to City Point and Fort Monroe, Virginia. *Library of Congress.*

It was able to carry up to 150 passengers as determined by the certificate of inspection it held.[35] *Massachusetts* remained under charter until June 10, 1865, when it returned to passenger service duty. Overall, it earned $48,634.06 while in government service.

The use of vessels as troop transports began in 1861 and was reported in an article in the *Baltimore Sun*,[36] which stated that the "rumors of movement of troops" were verified by the presence of a number of steamers in the local waters. These first transports were carrying Sherman's Battery, five companies of infantry from Texas and a regiment out of Pennsylvania. As the war progressed, more and more vessels were needed to move the troops from place to place. They became particularly important during General George B. McClellan's Peninsula Campaign in 1862, which was the first large-scale offensive movement in the Eastern Theater. These troop transports carried more than 120,000 soldiers to Hampton, Virginia, where they gathered for a unified march on Richmond. By the end of the war, transport vessels were running daily between Washington and the army's headquarters at City Point, Virginia, carrying passengers and mail. Other vessels in the transport fleet carried supplies, cavalry and artillery horses and mules out of Washington and broken down and otherwise unserviceable equipment and animals back to Washington for repair or disposal.

CHAPTER 4

THE ASSASSINATION OF PRESIDENT ABRAHAM LINCOLN

Search all vessels going out of the river for the assassins. Detain all suspicious persons. Guard against all crossing of the river and touching of vessels or boats on the Virginia shore.
—Navy Department telegram, April 17, 1865, from Gideon Welles, secretary of the navy, to Commander F.A. Parker, U.S. Navy, commanding Potomac Flotilla, St. Inigoes, Maryland

In April 1865, following the assassination of President Abraham Lincoln, the largest manhunt to that time in American history began. It involved men from all branches of the service, working cooperatively with a single purpose. The hunt focused on Southern Maryland, which had come under immediate suspicion and was an obvious place for the assassins to receive aid.

On Friday, April 14, John Wilkes Booth shot President Abraham Lincoln while he was watching the play *Our American Cousin* at Ford's Theater in Washington, D.C. At that same time, George Atzerodt was to kill Vice President Andrew Johnson and Lewis Powell was to murder Secretary of State William Seward. They were all to meet on the Maryland side of the Navy Yard Bridge and ride south together. Powell was unfamiliar with the city, so Booth had assigned David Herold to guide him to Seward's home and then out of the city to Maryland, to the rendezvous point. Only Booth was successful.

The next day, Commander Parker received word at his headquarters at St. Inigoes, Maryland, that the assassins might attempt to escape across the Potomac River. General James Barnes, commander of the District of St. Mary's, received word at Point Lookout on Saturday night that he was to permit no boats to leave until further notice. He responded by wire at 11:20 a.m. and wrote that he had received the dispatched orders and had immediately communicated them to the gunboats, so the Potomac River and Chesapeake Bay were being closely watched. The Military District of St. Mary's, established in 1863, was also being thoroughly patrolled by mounted men.[37]

Major General Christopher Augur, in command of Washington, D.C.'s defenses, sent Lieutenant David Dana and a troop from the Thirteenth New York Cavalry into Southern Maryland with orders to search for Booth and arrest anyone who appeared suspicious. He set up headquarters at the Bryantown Tavern, which was being operated by James Montgomery. Lieutenant Alexander Lovett of the Veteran Reserve Corps was sent to join Dana on the eighteenth, with military detectives Simon Gavacon, Joshua Lloyd and William Williams. They were later joined by General Winfield Scott Hancock, who made the tavern his headquarters.

Abner Hard, a member of the Eighth Illinois Cavalry, which was ordered to Leonardtown in St. Mary's County on the night of the assassination, wrote, "The country is so thoroughly picketed and searched, that a rabbit could have hardly made his escape through our lines without being discovered." Hard also mentioned that the local citizens were reluctant to provide any information.[38] The Illinois Cavalry was joined by the Sixteenth Regiment New York Volunteer Cavalry as well. This group ultimately rode into Virginia in response to Federal intelligence information.

On Sunday, April 16, Secretary of the Navy Gideon Welles sent out a telegram to Commander Parker, alerting him that John Wilkes Booth had been traced to Upper Marlboro on the Patuxent River, so he was to carefully guard that river and the Maryland coast from Point Lookout to Baltimore. The Potomac Flotilla was to search all vessels it encountered on the river and prevent any from reaching the Virginia shore.[39] The commanding officer of naval forces in Hampton Roads, Virginia, also received a telegram from Welles telling him to send any vessels that may be currently unemployed to the flotilla.[40]

In response, Parker sent ten gunboats and armed sloops to patrol the Potomac River from Mattawoman Creek to the mouth, with orders to seize all boats. Lieutenant Commander Eastman was assigned that duty on *Don* along with "such other boats as I [Parker] could spare from the Potomac." He assigned another ten gunboats to cruise the bay between Point Lookout

THE ASSASSINATION.

The Accomplices in Maryland.—The Disloyalists to be punished.—War Department Washington, April 22 1865.—Major Gen Dix, New York:—The counties of Prince George's, Charles and St. Mary's, have, during the whole war, been noted for hostility to the government and their protection to rebel blockade-runners, rebel spies, and every species of of public enemy. The murderers of the President harbored there before the murder, and Booth fled in that direction. If he escapes, it will be owing to rebel accomplices in that region. The military commander of the department will speedily take measures to bring these rebel sympathizers and accomplices in the murder to a sense of their criminal conduct.

E. M. Stanton,
Secretary of War.

St. Mary's Beacon, April 27, 1865.

and the Eastern Shore, intercepting all boats bound down the bay. He sent four fast boats to cruise along the Maryland coast from Annapolis to Point Lookout and seven boats to guard the coast of Virginia from Point Lookout to the York River. The monitor *Chime* was to remain at anchor at Point Lookout, and *Stepping Stones* was to carry provisions to the fleet.

Two days later, on Tuesday the nineteenth, Commander Parker received a telegram from St. Inigoes, informing him that the picket guard he had established inland of the supply depot there had been fired on twice the previous night. He therefore ordered the guard doubled and had all boats on the St. Mary's River seized. All boats seized by the flotilla were taken to their headquarters depot at St. Inigoes. Some were destroyed, and others were offered back to their owners in July 1865, if the owner would appear and swear an oath that he had been loyal during the rebellion. None who came forward to claim their property would swear the oath, so the vessels were ultimately distributed among officers, seamen and pilots who had served faithfully during the rebellion and to some contrabands who had acted as guides.[41]

Commander Parker felt that the Potomac River and Chesapeake Bay were being vigilantly guarded but stated in a letter to Secretary Welles that "twice the number of boats constituting the Potomac Flotilla could not prevent a canoe from crossing at night from Maryland to Virginia." He went on to say that it was for that reason that he had suggested to the secretary of war that a large cavalry force be sent to reconnoiter on the Northern Neck of Virginia. A force of just one hundred men was sent to the Coan River, so Parker called for more boats, intending to fill in the gaps between vessels to form a blockade, making it impossible for even the smallest boat to escape notice.

By then, as Commander Parker was establishing his picket line of vessels, the assassin John Wilkes Booth and his co-conspirator David Herold[42] were hiding in the swamps of Charles County, Maryland, waiting for the right moment to cross the Potomac River into Virginia. They were being aided by Thomas Jones and Samuel Cox, both Confederate agents working in Southern Maryland. On Friday, April 21, Jones was at the village of Allen's Fresh when John R. Walton, a local man who was serving as a guide for a Federal cavalry unit, came in and said, "I have news that those fellows have been seen down in St. Mary's County." Jones knew this would pull the troops out of Charles County, so at dusk, he went to where Booth and Herold were hiding and told them the time had come for them to cross into Virginia. It was a damp and cloudy night, with a gray fog rising from the marsh below the village. The wind was calm but had been blowing all day, and there was a swell on the river due to the flood tide.[43]

At about 10:00 p.m., the two conspirators took Jones's skiff and started on their way. But a strong flood tide carried them upstream and forced them back to the Maryland shore, approximately twelve miles north of where they had started, near the home of John J. Hughes, a Confederate sympathizer who was known to Herold. Shortly after Booth and Herold started across the river, the USS *Juniper*,[44] a gunboat that served the flotilla as a tug, dispatch vessel and patrol ship, put down anchor off Persimmon Point and reported in its log that at about 11:45 p.m. a wind began to blow from the south.[45]

The next day, Saturday the twenty-second, while Booth and Herold were resting from their first attempt to cross the Potomac River and waiting for a second chance, three hundred Union soldiers were marching from Camp Parole, Maryland, to Alexandria, Virginia, to board a troop transport the next day. And Captain Lee, assistant quartermaster, Alexandria Depot, was looking for vessels and men to send to the middle Potomac to join the flotilla and keep Booth's crossing from happening. Captain Lee was reacting to a request from Commander Parker, who had been alerted by Gideon Welles to Booth's presence. The telegram stated that Booth had been near Bryantown on the previous Saturday (April 15), where Dr. Mudd had set his broken leg bone and went on to say, "The utmost vigilance is necessary in the Potomac and Patuxent to prevent his escape. All boats should be searched" until further notice.[46] But they were too late; Booth and Herold were successful on their second attempt and arrived on the Virginia shore early Sunday morning.

By this time, only Lafayette Baker and Major O'Beirne, with their squads of detectives, had determined that Booth and Herold had already crossed into Virginia. This was confirmed while searching in lower Maryland, where they found witnesses, including an old Black man who told them the two had crossed the Potomac, near Matthews Point, on Saturday night, the twenty-second of April. O'Beirne thus took his forces across the Potomac in pursuit.

CHAPTER 5

THE MEN

The effects of rebel treatment will follow most of us to our graves.
—letter from Robert Kellogg to his father and mother, May 11, 1865

One of the vessels that answered Captain Lee's call was the *Black Diamond*, which carried a crew of five under normal circumstances, including Captain Couch and Engineer Husted. When it received special orders from Captain Allen, assistant quartermaster, on April 22, 1865, an additional ten men plus one captain were taken on for guard duty. Husted said that "the ten men belonged to the Volunteer Fire Department of Alexandria, Virginia,"[47] and had volunteered to join this mission. Captain Lee also referred to them as members of the Third Regiment, Quartermaster Volunteers. All reportedly volunteered to go on this guard duty mission, perhaps lured by thoughts of the reward being offered for the capture of John Wilkes Booth and the other conspirators. While serving on the *Black Diamond*, these men were employed and paid by the Quartermaster Department as civilian employees, not military personnel. Three of the four men whose names are known were blacksmiths; the fourth was a carpenter. One of the blacksmiths was a resident of Fairfax County, Virginia, and lived just outside Alexandria. The others appear to have come from eastern Pennsylvania.

The transport *Massachusetts* was making one of its standard runs between Alexandria and the Union stronghold at Fort Monroe, carrying Federal soldiers. On the way, it stopped at General Grant's headquarters depot at City Point, Virginia, to pick up supplies and sometimes drop off or pick up

Charleston, S. C., C. S. America,
September, 1864.

"We, the undersigned, prisoners of war, confined in the city of Charleston, in the Confederate States of America, do pledge our parole individually as military men and men of honor, that we will not attempt to pass the lines which shall be established and guarded around our prison house; nor will we, by letter, word, or sign, hold any intercourse with parties beyond those lines, nor with those who may visit us, without authority. It is understood by us, that this parole is voluntary on our part, and given in consideration of privileges secured to us, by lessening the stringency of the guard, of free ingress and egress of the house and appointed grounds during the day, by which we secure a liberty of fresh air and exercise, grateful to comfort and health.

"Hereby we admit that this, our parole, binds us in letter and spirit, with no room for doubts or technicality of construction, and its violation will be an act of lasting disgrace. Signed:"

This oath was signed by prisoners of war when they were paroled and waiting to be exchanged. *By the author.*

additional passengers. From Fort Monroe, the troops would either transfer to another oceangoing vessel for the remainder of their journey or march overland. The men on this trip were to rejoin their regiments to complete their terms of service before mustering out or would be continuing service as part of the occupying forces in the South.

Most of the men on the *Massachusetts* were recently paroled prisoners of war, mostly from Andersonville, Georgia, but a few had also been held in Danville and Richmond, Virginia. All had been sent to Camp Parole, Maryland, to prepare for their exchange and return to duty. A few others were returning from hospital stays and extended medical furloughs.

In the early years of the war, soldiers who were captured were held by their captors until an exchange could be arranged. But as the numbers of prisoners grew, the military had no choice but to parole them home. The soldiers had their names entered onto a list, swore an oath to not take up arms again until exchanged and were sent home to wait for the call to return to duty. This was known as parole d'honneur ("word of honor") and was a long-standing military tradition. It soon became necessary to exchange prisoners right on the battlefields, as there was nowhere to keep the large number of men being captured.

There was no centralized system or set of rules, and it soon became clear that once home, the soldiers were not inclined to return to their units when called, and some simply could not be found.

To resolve this issue, parole camps and official exchange sites were established in July 1862. All soldiers currently on parole at home were now required to report to a parole camp. The first three holding places were Camp of Instruction (later Camp Parole), Annapolis, Maryland; Camp Chase, Columbus, Ohio; and Jefferson Barracks, Missouri. Men were to report to the camps based on their home states in order to facilitate furloughs home. New Englanders and those from the Mid-Atlantic reported to Maryland; men from Virginia, Tennessee, Kentucky, Ohio, Indiana and Michigan reported to Ohio; and men from Illinois, Wisconsin, Minnesota, Iowa and Missouri reported to Missouri. Anyone who did not report was counted a deserter. Aiken's Landing, Virginia, and Vicksburg, Mississippi, were designated as the official exchange sites.

At these camps, the soldiers were kept under military discipline and in a known place, where they could be found when called on and returned to their units when they had been officially exchanged. Union General Ulysses S. Grant ordered a cessation of prisoner exchanges in April 1864, allowing only sick and wounded soldiers to be released that fall, without needing to be exchanged. General Grant felt that continuing to exchange prisoners and send them back into the lines would prolong the war and that the South could be subdued more efficiently through attrition. In an

All soldiers from the Mid-Atlantic states were sent to Camp Parole, Annapolis, Maryland, when released from prison camp and waiting to be exchanged. *Library of Congress.*

August 18 dispatch to General Butler, he wrote, "It is hard on our men held in Southern prisons not to exchange them, but it is humanity to those left in the ranks to fight our battles. Every man released on parole or otherwise becomes an active soldier against us at once, either directly or indirectly. If we commence a system of exchange which liberates all prisoners taken, we will have to fight on until the whole South is exterminated." This was also in reaction to proposed mistreatment of Black prisoners by their Confederate captors. The exchanges began again in earnest in January 1865.

The camps were guarded by Union troops and fell under the general jurisdiction of the local provost marshal. At Camp Parole, that was Captain Troch. Nurses serving there at that time included Clara Barton.

Fifteen of the twenty-nine men who have been identified as lost from the *Massachusetts* came from regiments captured at Plymouth, North Carolina, on April 20, 1864. They were from Connecticut, Massachusetts, New York and Pennsylvania.

The 1864 Battle of Plymouth was the last major victory for the Confederacy. Union forces had taken the town in May 1862 and had been using it as a base for raids all over eastern North Carolina. But with the help of the ironclads *Albemarle* and *Neuse*, Confederate General Robert Hoke laid siege to the town in the spring of 1864 and captured it—along with 2,364 Union soldiers.

The battle began on April 17, a bright and beautiful day. The Union soldiers lay in camp, none expecting an attack, "but ere the day closed we were surrounded by twelve thousand Confederate soldiers under General Robert F. Hoke, CSA, our little garrison numbering all told about 2,000 men."[48] By noon on April 20, the entire garrison of Plymouth was in the hands of the Rebels, and all the captured were concentrated on the Washington Road, the main road out of town. They were relieved of their arms and equipment and issued four days' worth of rations before settling in for the night. About noon on the twenty-first their march began and lasted until about nine o'clock that evening. They had come a distance of thirteen miles, escorted by the Thirty-Fifth North Carolina Regiment. They marched more or less every day until noon of the twenty-fifth, when they arrived at the railhead at Tarboro, North Carolina, where the Seventh North Carolina Regiment took over guard duty. At this point, the officers were separated from their men.[49] Rations were distributed and included raw meat, beans and bacon. Some of the townswomen traded cooking pots and more food in exchange for any greenbacks or clothing the soldiers had and were willing to trade.

MEMORANDUM FROM PRISONER OF WAR RECORDS. No. 97

(This blank to be used only in the arrangement of said records.)

NAME.	RANK.	No. of Reg't.	State.	Arm of Service.	Co.	Records of—
Krepps William	P	140	Pa	[illegible]	[illegible]	[illegible]

Captured at Cold Harbor June 2, 1864, confined at Richmond, Va., June 5, 186

Sent to Andersonville June 8/64. Reconfined at Richmond March 12/65

Admitted to Hospital at Richmond Va. Mar 12/65 [illegible] age 23.

where he died , 186 , of

Paroled at Cox's Wharf Mar 10, 1865; reported at Camp Parole, Md., [illegible], 186

Arrived at C.G.B. Mar 13/65 sent to C.P. Mar 15/65 arrived at C.P. Mar 17/65

Clothing Mar 13/65

Copied by (over)

MEMORANDUM FROM PRISONER OF WAR RECORDS. No.

(This blank to be used only in the arrangement of said records.)

NAME.	RANK.	No. of Reg't.	State.	Arm of Service.	Co.	Records of—
Murphy Thos.	P.	59	Mass.	Inf.	B.	OR Ex

Captured at Petersburg Va. July 30, 1864, confined at Richmond, Va., [illegible] Feby 20, 1865.

Admitted to Hospital at Danville Va. Jany [illegible]

where he died , 186 , of

Paroled at James River Va. Feb. 22, 1865; reported at Camp Parole, Md., , 186 .

Copied by A.A.

Top: Prisoner of war record for William Krepps, one of the soldiers lost in the collision. *National Archives and Records Administration.*

Bottom: Prisoner of war record for Thomas Murphy, one of the soldiers lost in the collision. *National Archives and Records Administration.*

The men were held in the stock pens at Tarboro until the morning of April 29, when they marched to the depot to take the railroad cars to Camp Sumter, Andersonville, Georgia, where, as their captors informed them, rations would be "dealt out plenteously." Each time they boarded a train, a special notice was given to the president of the line, informing him of the number of prisoners to be moved, approximately when they wanted to board and where they were to be taken.

They were crowded aboard small railroad boxcars, and six Rebel guards were stationed in each car, barring the door. They arrived at daybreak at Wilmington, North Carolina, where they received more rations of bacon and hardtack. There they crossed the river by ferryboats and proceeded to Florence, South Carolina. From there, they rode another train to Charleston, South Carolina, arriving there on May 1. There they were greeted by many sympathetic citizens who gave them cigars and food, taking nothing in exchange.

After another change of cars was made—this time onto open cars—they left Charleston by rail at 7:00 a.m. and arrived at Savannah, Georgia, at 2:00 p.m. There they changed trains again and proceeded to Macon, Georgia. They finally reached Camp Sumter at Andersonville, Georgia, at 9:00 p.m. the next evening, May 2, 1864.[50] There they were counted off in detachments that numbered 270 men each. These detachments were further ordered into messes of 90 men each, which aided in the distribution of the scant rations they received.

The officers took the same journey but were not supposed to be at Camp Sumter, so they were held in a church outside the prison overnight and boarded the trains again the next morning, after attending morning church service. (Troops and transports took "Sabbath layovers" on Sunday morning when possible.) The officers were heading back to Macon, Georgia, and Camp Oglethorpe. Officers from the Plymouth engagement who had initially been sent to Libby Prison in Richmond, Virginia, arrived at Camp Oglethorpe the following day.

During their five arduous months in Andersonville, they watched fellow soldiers die of disease and starvation; get beaten to death by their fellow prisoners over a scrap a food, a watch or a piece of firewood; and be shot by a guard for stepping over the dead line, whether intentionally or by accident. They came to hate those prisoners who agreed to work for the guards for an extra morsel of food. These last they considered traitors and hoped they would be recognized as such and not exchanged when the time came. And they heard many rumors and suffered many disappointments about when their paroles and exchanges would come.[51] Finally, on September 1, they were taken out of Andersonville and began their long journey north. They were first sent to Charleston, South Carolina, where they were held at the fairgrounds and old racecourse. They were heading for Florence, South Carolina, where they were to spend the winter months, but they had to layover in Charleston until the pens were completed at Florence. While in Charleston, they witnessed the shelling of the town by the Union gunboats in the harbor[52] and suffered a yellow fever epidemic that raged through the prison guard forces.

The men arrived at Florence on October 2, and paroles began to be written for the sick and wounded on November 1. These men were sent

The men captured at the Battle of Plymouth, North Carolina, were held in the prison at Florence, South Carolina, while making their way north after being paroled out of Andersonville Prison in Georgia. James E. Taylor created a series of drawings while there. *Library of Congress.*

to Charleston at the rate of about two thousand a day. They traveled from Charleston onboard the transport *Verona*. They left there about sunset on December 14 and reached Fort Monroe about 1:00 a.m. on December 16, having "made good time up the Chesapeake Bay in a smooth sea." They made Annapolis, Maryland, just before dark and were mustered in the next day.[53]

By mid-February 1865, they were all paroled, but overall, the losses in prison were nearly 50 percent for those who served time in Andersonville. Once paroled, they were sent north to Aiken's Landing, on the James River in Virginia, where they then traveled by steamer to Annapolis and then marched to Camp Parole nearby. There they were to wait for their exchange and their return to their regiments.

The officers were released from their prisons in the spring of 1865 and on March 2 took the steamer *General Sedgwick* to Annapolis, where they remained a week and received two months' back pay and a thirty-day leave of absence. When they returned from furlough, they were to report to Camp Parole.

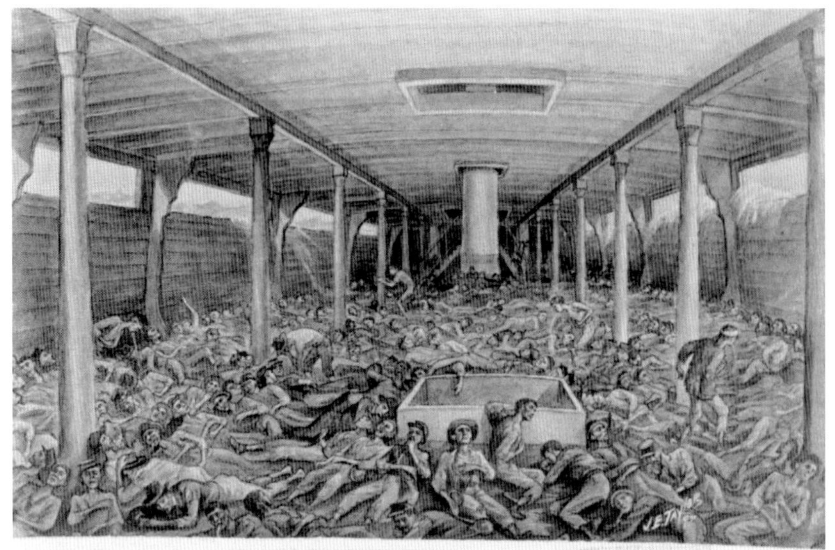

Florence Military Prison-Series.

"On board the old transport."

On Board the Old Transport by James E. Taylor shows recently released prisoners traveling north on a governmental troop transport. *Library of Congress.*

Most of the enlisted men held in Danville and Richmond had been captured during the Siege of Petersburg, Virginia; some at Cold Harbor, Virginia; others at Monocacy, Maryland; and one by John Singleton Mosby near Newtown, Virginia. Cold Harbor was the last battle in the Overland Campaign and was a Confederate victory. This led Union General Ulysses S. Grant to abandon his plan to attack Richmond head-on and instead lay siege to Petersburg. This campaign was a series of engagements that lasted 292 days, from June 1864 until March 1865, and included the Battles of Weldon Railroad, Hatcher's Run, the Crater, Deep Bottom Run and Peebles Farm. The final result was a Union victory when Confederate General Robert E. Lee abandoned both Petersburg and Richmond and then surrendered his entire army just a few weeks later at Appomattox, Virginia. The Battle of Monocacy occurred that same summer and was part of the Confederate plan to capture Washington, D.C. Outnumbered three to one, the Federal forces were nonetheless victorious. In June 1864, John Singleton Mosby and his men were also in the Newtown, Virginia area, where they raided the rear guard of a Federal wagon train and captured a small group of men along with their horses and equipment.

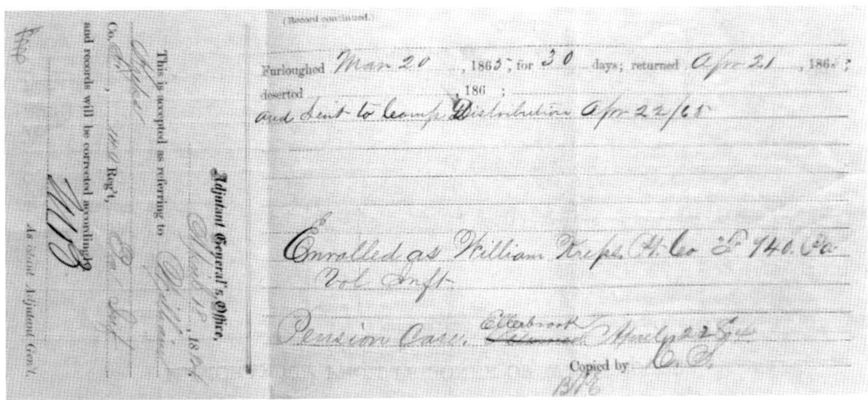
(Record continued.)

Furloughed Mar 20, 1865; for 30 days; returned Apr 21, 186 ;
deserted , 186 ;
and sent to Camp Distribution Apr 22/65

Enrolled as William [illegible] Co. H 140 Pa. Vol. Inft.

Pension Case,

Copied by

Adjutant General's Office,
, 186
This is accepted as referring to
Co. , Reg't,
and records will be corrected accordingly.
Assistant Adjutant Gen'l.

Once the paroled soldiers reached camp, they received their back pay and a pass for a thirty-day furlough. *Fold3.com.*

These men were all sent to Danville first. Located 140 miles west of Richmond, it was the supply base for the Confederate armies at Richmond and Petersburg. This complex consisted of six tobacco factories that had been converted for prison use in 1863. There they joined nearly two thousand other enlisted men and four hundred officers and were separated into divisions and mess squads, in the same way those in Andersonville were. Then in February 1865, 50 percent of the men being held there were transferred to Richmond due to overcrowding and disease; the others remained there until paroled.

During their time in Danville, the men were issued "scant rations in spite of being in the midst of plenty," as one soldier remembered. They made every effort to get some of the hardtack in storage but were told "no, that was for the Southern soldiers in the field." Their usual rations were cornbread and the heads of beef, when available.[54]

When they were exchanged, those coming out of Danville and Richmond were taken to Aiken's Landing, also known as Varina Landing, where they were met by ambulances to take those too feeble to walk the final six miles to the Union lines. After they disembarked, their places on the boats were taken by Confederate soldiers for whom they had been exchanged. While being transported, all of these men and the transports moved under a flag of truce and, whenever possible, with a medical officer and medical equipment on board.

Hundreds of released prisoners arrived at Camp Parole daily and weekly, according to the *Evening Star*, which reported on February 20, 1865, that 926 Union men had arrived from Richmond the previous day and that nearly

Aiken's Landing, Virginia, was established as the place for prisoner exchanges in the Eastern Theater. Prisoners in the Western Theater were exchanged in Vicksburg, Mississippi. *Library of Congress.*

3,000 had arrived there the previous week. Prison camps were emptying, and men were looking forward to returning to their units and ultimately their homes.

As soon as the soldiers arrived at the docks at the College Green Barracks in Annapolis, they were met by men and women of the Christian Commission, organized in 1861 to see to the needs of the men, physical and spiritual. These volunteers helped bury those who had perished during the journey north and helped move the others into the hospitals and camps. Soldiers waiting to be exchanged sometimes volunteered to assist the new arrivals, wanting to do something to help.

One member of the Christian Commission wrote:

> *Few points made memorable by the great war surpass in sad and tender interest Camp Parole and its neighboring hospitals and barracks at Annapolis. Here came the thousands, exchanged or waiting to be exchanged, from the terrible prisons at Richmond, Andersonville, and elsewhere.*[55]

The soldiers were given clothing by the Sanitary Commission, which was a civilian organization intent on bettering the living conditions of the Union army. They also had their hair and beards trimmed and were then taken to bathe. Their old clothes were steamed to kill bugs and disease and then sold for rags. Samual Grosvenor, Company B, Sixteenth Connecticut Volunteers, wrote in his diary on December 17, 1864: "[I] had a splendid bath, after which I put on my new clothing and felt the most comfortable I had for the longest time."[56] They were then divided into battalions and brought into the camp itself, officers still separated from the enlisted men. The Pennsylvania troops were all in the First Battalion; New York, New Jersey, Delaware and Maryland troops were in the Second Battalion; all New England troops were in the Third; and the western troops made up the Fourth. Each battalion had a commanding officer from among the soldiers permanently stationed at the camp. Colonel A.R. Root, of the Ninth New York Veteran Reserve Volunteers, commanded the post overall.[57]

While at Camp Parole, the men were nursed back to enough of a state of health that they could be returned to their different regiments and complete their terms of service. Most found the time in camp to be lazy, with nothing to do but draw their back pay and rations. Those too ill or injured to remain in camp were sent to area hospitals. All were given a thirty-day furlough, and some also received an additional ten-day "voter's furlough."[58]

When fit enough, and after their thirty-day furlough, the soldiers were moved to either the Washington Navy Yard or Camp Distribution, Alexandria, Virginia, for transport back to their units. According to the military officials, if a man was able to travel, he was fit for duty and must go to Camp Parole and prepare to rejoin his regiment.

Each removal of soldiers from Camp Parole was done under a special order, which specified where they were to be taken and under whose command. The group that ultimately boarded the *Massachusetts* went to Camp Distribution, which was a six-hour march from Camp Parole.

The camp in Alexandria was originally called Camp Convalescent and was used to house soldiers who were too ill to return to the field but not ill enough to warrant a hospital bed. In 1863, a new hospital camp was erected nearby, and the original site became a distribution center from which men fit for field service were sent back to their regiments. In 1864, the name was changed again, from Camp Distribution to Rendezvous of Distribution.

There was one man, John Hall, of the Twenty-Fifth Massachusetts Infantry, who was on the *Massachusetts* but had never been held prisoner. He had an incised wound on his right knee and was sent to the Third Division, Second Army Corps Depot Field Hospital at City Point, Virginia, on March 15, 1865. He was transferred to Harewood United States Army General Hospital in Washington, D.C., on March 28, having developed jaundice. He

MEN WANTED
FOR THE
INVALID CORPS.

Only those faithful soldiers who, from wounds or the hardships of war, are no longer fit for active field duty will be received in this Corps of Honor. Enlistments will be for three years, unless sooner discharged. Pay and allowances same as for officers and men of the United States Infantry; except that no premiums or bounties for enlistment will be allowed. This will not invalidate any pensions or bounties which may be due for previous services.

The following UNIFORM has been adopted for Officers and Men of the Invalid Corps:

FOR OFFICERS. FROCK COAT, of sky-blue cloth, with dark-blue velvet collar and cuffs; in all other respects, according to the present pattern for officers of infantry. SHOULDER STRAPS, according to present regulations, but worked on dark-blue velvet. PANTALOONS, of sky-blue cloth, with double stripe of dark-blue cloth down the outer seam, each stripe one-half inch wide, with space between of three-eighths of an inch. FORAGE CAP, present regulation.

FOR ENLISTED MEN. JACKET, of sky-blue kersey, with dark-blue trimmings, cut like the cavalry jacket, to come well down on the abdomen. TROWSERS, present regulation, sky-blue. FORAGE CAP, present regulation.

Men who are still in service and unable to perform effective field duty, may be transferred to this corps.

Medical Inspectors, Surgeons in charge of Hospitals, Military Commanders, and all others having authority to discharge, under existing laws and regulations, are forbidden to grant discharges to any men under their control who may be fit for service in the Invalid Corps.

For the convenience of service, the men will be selected for three grades of duty. Those who are most efficient and able-bodied, and capable of performing guard duty, etc., etc., will be armed with muskets, and assigned to companies of the First Battalion. Those of the next degree of efficiency, including those who have lost a hand or an arm; and the least effective, including those who have lost a foot or leg, to the companies of the Second or Third Battalions; they will be armed with swords.

The duties will be chiefly to act as provost guards and garrisons for cities; guards for hospitals and other public buildings; and as clerks, orderlies, etc. If found necessary, they may be assigned to forts, etc.

Acting Assistant Provost-Marshals General are authorized to appoint Officers of the Regular Service, or of the Invalid Corps, to administer the oath of enlistment to those men who have completely fulfilled the prescribed conditions of admission to the Invalid Corps, viz: 1—That the applicant is unfit for service in the field. 2—That he is fit for the duties, or some of them, indicated above. 3—That, if not now in the service, he was honorably discharged. 4—That he is meritorious and deserving.

For enlistment or further information, apply to the Board of Enrolment for the District in which the applicant is a resident.

Disabled Soldiers who are residents of the Seventh Congressional District, who desire admission into the Invalid Corps, are requested to present themselves to the Board of Enrolment

ON TUESDAY AND FRIDAY AFTERNOONS,

From 2 to 5 o'clock, on which days the Board will be in session for the purpose of examining applicants, and granting certificates to those who have fulfilled the prescribed conditions of admission.

S. BENTON THOMPSON, Captain and Provost-Marshal,
ADDISON G. FAY, Commissioner of Enrolment,
DAVID S. FOGG, Surgeon, } *Board of Enrolment.*

CONCORD, June 15, 1863.

FROM WRIGHT & POTTER'S BOSTON PRINTING ESTABLISHMENT, No. 4 SPRING LANE, CORNER OF DEVONSHIRE STREET.

was discharged on April 22 and was to return to his regiment. But unlike the others on board, he was going only as far as City Point, as his unit was still in Virginia, having participated in the surrender in Appomattox on April 9.

Once on board the transport vessels, the men were divided into detachments or companies depending on their numbers, much as they were in Camp Parole, in accordance with the regulations specified in Special Order No. 276, issued on August 8, 1863.[59] The order said that an officer was to organize the troops into detachments or companies "and take all

Opposite: The Invalid Corps was organized in 1863 and made up of disabled soldiers who were still able to serve, just not necessarily on the front lines. Before the end of the war, the name was changed to the Veteran Reserve Corps. *Wikimedia Commons.*

Right: The Sixteenth Connecticut Infantry Regiment lost more men in the collision than any other known unit. *By the author.*

ENGAGEMENTS.

Antietam, Md.—September 17th, 1862. Loss in killed, four commissioned officers, 38 enlisted men; wounded, eight commissioned officers, 176 enlisted men; captured, 12 enlisted men; *Total Loss*, 238.

Fredericksburg, Virginia.—December 12, 13, and 14, 1862. Loss in wounded, one enlisted man. *Total loss one.*

Edenton Road, Suffolk, Virginia.—April 24, 1863. Loss in killed, one enlisted man; wounded, seven enlisted men. *Total loss, eight.*

Providence Church Road, Suffolk, Virginia.—May 3, 1863. Loss in killed, two enlisted men; wounded, one commissioned officer, seven enlisted men. *Total loss*, 10.

Plymouth, North Carolina.—April 20, 1864. Loss in killed, one enlisted man; wounded, one commissioned officer, 11 enlisted men; captured, 23 commissioned officers, 400 enlisted men. *Total loss* 436.

CASUALTIES.

Killed in action,	47
Died of wounds,	45
Died of disease,	73
Died in prison,	177
Shot in prison,	1
Supposed shot while attempting to escape from prison,	1
Lost at sea from burning steamship "General Lyon,"	1
Drowned from accident,	1
Drowned from collision of "Black Diamond," on Potomac river.	7
Total deaths,	353

measures necessary to put his command into the best state of efficiency to meet any emergency." The order further stipulated that when soldiers from a variety of units were being transported without benefit of their own officers, an officer was to be assigned in order to "secure and preserve discipline." Captain James Holmes of the Third Regiment, Veteran Reserve Corps, was the officer put in command of the army personnel on board the *Massachusetts* for this trip.

The Veteran Reserve Corps had been organized by the War Department on April 28, 1863, under General Order No. 105, as the Invalid Corps and was made up of disabled soldiers who were still able to serve in some capacity. These soldiers were among the last of the Federal troops to be mustered out of service. At this time, members of the Veteran Reserve Corps were being used almost exclusively to escort prisoners during exchanges and as officers on board troop transport vessels.

CHAPTER 6

THE INCIDENT

It was a clear night, but moonless....A strong wind began to blow, and the river became very rough.
—George Hollands of the 101st Pennsylvania Volunteer Infantry

On Sunday morning, April 23, 1865, Captain Allen of the Washington, D.C. Quartermaster Depot gave the *Black Diamond* special orders to report to the Naval Depot at Piney Point, Maryland, where it would receive further instructions about joining the Potomac Flotilla. This was in response to the news that Booth was near Bryantown, which resulted in a request for "utmost vigilance...in the Potomac and Patuxent to prevent his escape."[60] The word of the $100,000 reward ($1,931,000 in 2024) was to be spread among the people as well.[61] When the *Black Diamond* set off downriver, the weather that morning was sultry, with a "northwest wind which...brought out the sun."[62]

Captain Meredith and his vessel left Alexandria in mid-morning and traveled the ninety-two miles to Piney Point, arriving at 11:00 p.m. There they received orders to join the picket line and prevent Booth and Herold from crossing the river. They steamed back up the Potomac River thirteen miles and reached their duty station, which was within a mile of Blackistone Island, at approximately 12:35 a.m. on April 24. They anchored there for the night, nearly opposite the Blackistone Lighthouse. The *Black Diamond* was showing the single light as required by maritime law. It was a clear night, but dark, the moon having set.[63]

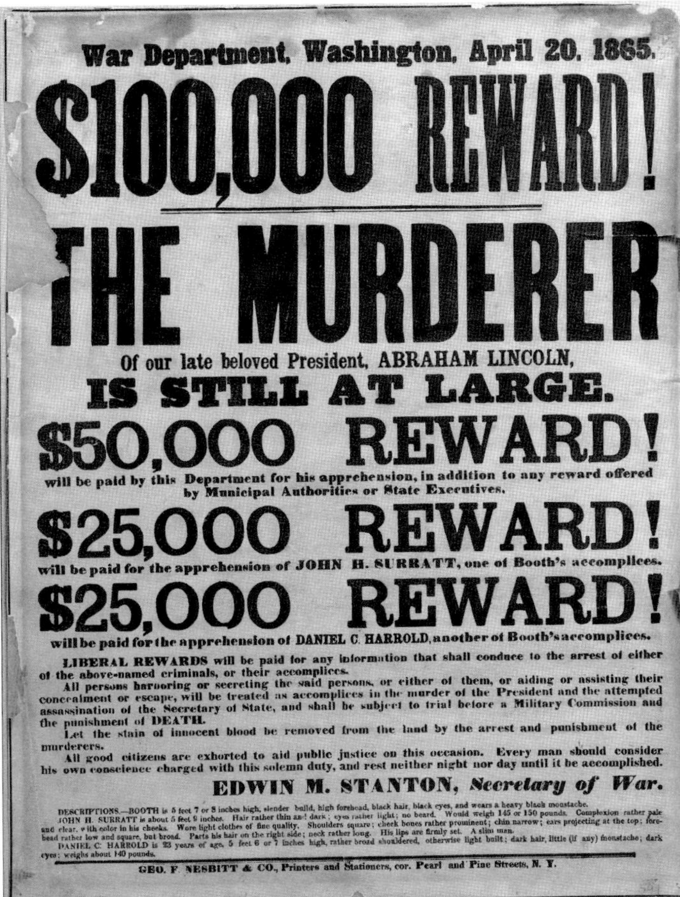

War Department, Washington, April 20, 1865.

$100,000 REWARD!

THE MURDERER

Of our late beloved President, ABRAHAM LINCOLN,

IS STILL AT LARGE.

$50,000 REWARD!

will be paid by this Department for his apprehension, in addition to any reward offered by Municipal Authorities or State Executives.

$25,000 REWARD!

will be paid for the apprehension of JOHN H. SURRATT, one of Booth's accomplices.

$25,000 REWARD!

will be paid for the apprehension of DANIEL C. HARROLD, another of Booth's accomplices.

LIBERAL REWARDS will be paid for any information that shall conduce to the arrest of either of the above-named criminals, or their accomplices.

All persons harboring or secreting the said persons, or either of them, or aiding or assisting their concealment or escape, will be treated as accomplices in the murder of the President and the attempted assassination of the Secretary of State, and shall be subject to trial before a Military Commission and the punishment of DEATH.

Let the stain of innocent blood be removed from the land by the arrest and punishment of the murderers.

All good citizens are exhorted to aid public justice on this occasion. Every man should consider his own conscience charged with this solemn duty, and rest neither night nor day until it be accomplished.

EDWIN M. STANTON, *Secretary of War.*

DESCRIPTIONS.—BOOTH is 5 feet 7 or 8 inches high, slender build, high forehead, black hair, black eyes, and wears a heavy black moustache.
JOHN H. SURRATT is about 5 feet 9 inches. Hair rather thin and dark; eyes rather light; no beard. Would weigh 145 or 150 pounds. Complexion rather pale and clear, with color in his cheeks. Wore light clothes of fine quality. Shoulders square; cheek bones rather prominent; chin narrow; ears projecting at the top; forehead rather low and square, but broad. Parts his hair on the right side; neck rather long. His lips are firmly set. A slim man.
DANIEL C. HARROLD is 23 years of age, 5 feet 6 or 7 inches high, rather broad shouldered, otherwise light built; dark hair, little (if any) moustache; dark eyes; weighs about 140 pounds.

GEO. F. NESBITT & CO., Printers and Stationers, cor. Pearl and Pine Streets, N. Y.

Left: Secretary of War Edwin Stanton put forth rewards for the capture of John Wilkes Booth and his fellow conspirators. *Library of Congress.*

Below: At the time of the collision the sky was very dark. The sliver of the moon had set and was well below the horizon. *In-the-sky.org.*

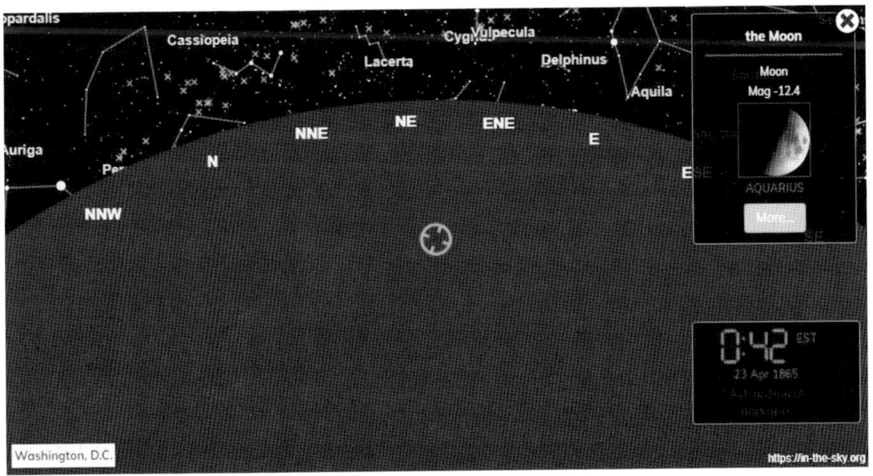

Regulations for Preventing Collisions on the Water
An Act of the 38th Congress | April 29, 1864

lights for ships at anchor
Article 7. Ships, whether steamships or sailing-ships, when at anchor in roadsteads or fairways, shall, between sunset and sunrise, exhibit where it can best be seen, but at a height not exceeding twenty feet above the hull, a white light in a globular lantern of eight inches in diameter, and so constructed as to show a clear uniform and unbroken light visible all around the horizon, and at a distance of at least one mile.

Captain Couch, with the troop transport steamer *Massachusetts*, set sail south out of Alexandria, Virginia, at 5:00 p.m. on that same Sunday evening. The water was calm, and they were showing the required running lights. They were bound for City Point and Fort Monroe, Virginia. On board were approximately three hundred Federal soldiers from a variety of regiments—nearly twice as many as the ship was approved to carry. The men were to change ships in City Point, boarding an oceangoing vessel that would take them to the Union stronghold at Newbern,[64] North Carolina, either through the Albemarle and Chesapeake Canal to Roanoke Island or via the outer route around Cape Hatteras, depending on the season of the year. There they would rejoin their regiments to serve out their enlistments.

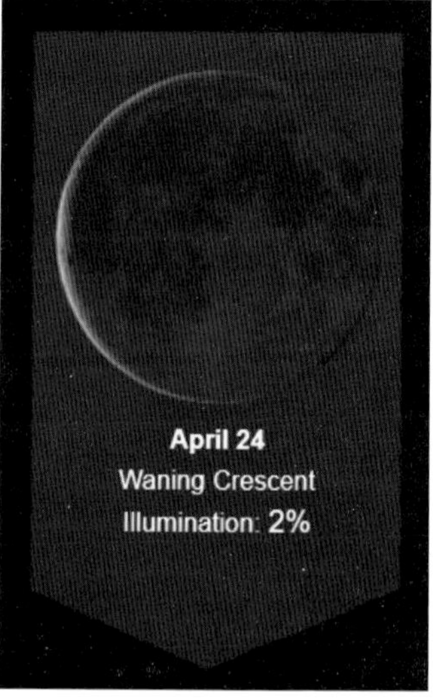

The night of the collision, the moon was a waning crescent so gave off only 2 percent of its full light capacity. *In-the-sky.org*.

As the trip continued, the wind picked up and the waters became very rough shortly after dark. Veterans of the 101st Pennsylvania Volunteer Infantry, traveling on the *Massachusetts*, recalled that the vessel was traveling downriver "quite nicely" until a strong wind began to blow, causing the river to become rough. The soldiers on board later related that they were not very confident of their vessel's condition in the rough water, as it was old and not very fit.

The moon, which was just a waning crescent, had set and was well below the horizon, making the night very dark. The men on board were sleeping, many on the open deck, when they were awakened by a jolt and loud noise. Some were thrown overboard by the impact.

Traveling past Blackistone Island, shortly before 1:00 a.m., the *Massachusetts* struck the *Black Diamond* on its port side near the boiler, just aft of the wheelhouse, and opened its iron hull right down to the waterline. The *Massachusetts* also sustained some damage, but it was not severe. Its bows were stove in above the waterline, leaving a hole "large enough to take in five or six men abreast," according to survivor William Nott, Company K, Sixteenth Connecticut.[65]

In the dark, all became panic and confusion. Many men on board the *Massachusetts*, woken abruptly from their sleep, ran forward to see what had happened and found the bow filling with water. Some grabbed their coats, others their haversacks and equipment, and others went with just what they had been sleeping in. Captain Couch ordered all on board to the stern in order to raise the damaged bow out of the water and keep them afloat. Seeing the other boat close by and still apparently afloat, the men began shouting to it to come closer and rescue them.

According to a deposition by survivor George Peckham, Ninth New York Heavy Artillery, Company K, "It was announced in a loud tone by some officer on board the *Massachusetts* to go on board the other vessel."[66] Some complied, fearing that the *Massachusetts* was about to go under; some, like Peckham, stayed put and survived. He later said that was the only order he had ever disobeyed. Others jumped overboard into the water, grabbing planks and whatever they could find that would float.

The *Black Diamond* swung alongside, hoping to offload its crew onto the less-damaged vessel, but instead, about 150 of the men from the *Massachusetts* started jumping onto it, causing it to go down even faster. The men had assumed it was a relief boat and commenced to jump, "like a flock of sheep going over a wall after their leader."[67] In coming alongside, the *Black Diamond* smashed one of the *Massachusetts*'s lifeboats, rendering it unseaworthy and leaving only one boat to assist with the rescue efforts. After the *Black Diamond* disappeared beneath the waves, the *Massachusetts* stayed near the spot until daybreak, picking up about 100 survivors, in spite of the damage to its bow.

Many of the survivors later related tales of being in the water for three hours or more, clinging to any bit of debris they could find and listening to the cries for help coming from others who had fallen or jumped into the river. Others, like Peckham, wrote of watching their friends and fellow soldiers go down with the wrecked vessel.

The collision depicted in this painting by Angela M. Wathen occurred in the early morning hours of April 25, 1865. *St. Clement's Island Museum Division.*

The *Black Diamond*'s chief engineer, Joseph Husted, wrote that he "was endeavoring to save him [George W. Carter, drummer, Sixteenth Connecticut Infantry] but he was so benumbed that he could not catch hold of the line." He had first jumped onto the *Black Diamond*, but when it began to sink, he jumped into the water, floating with the help of a plank until about 2:00 a.m.[68]

Other survivors who remembered the incident also recounted this same story, including George Hollands, Company B, 101st Pennsylvania Volunteer Infantry. He wrote that Carter "grasped hold of the keel of the boat, or something else, and was hanging on for dear life and calling for help. One of the crew up in the rigging got hold of a rope and time and time again threw it to where the boy was, telling him to grab for it, but the boy couldn't get hold of it. Every now and then a wave would wash over him and strangle him, and as he would emerge from it, he would call for the rope. He finally became exhausted and cried out to us that he could hold out no longer.…He said he was a drummer of Co. D, 16th Connecticut and asked us to inform his mother that he was drowned. He bade us goodbye, saying, 'boys I must go' and as the next wave washed over him, he loosened his hold and sank beneath the waves."[69]

Today, the water temperature in the Potomac River in the vicinity of Blackistone Island averages from 48.9 to 60.35 degrees Fahrenheit in April. In 1865, these temperatures were even lower due to the harsher winters of the nineteenth century. And it had been rainy all week, according to the newspapers. There had been a frost in much of the area the night before, which the papers reported as being "an extraordinary change" in the weather, and it was most unpleasant. For swimmers, a temperature above 66 degrees is preferable. For these men, who were still recovering from prison camps and ill health, the ideal temperature was even higher. For the hardiest of swimmers, which most of these men were most definitely not, temperatures below 61 degrees feel bracingly cold and are both tolerable and safe for a quick dip. Those below 55 degrees feel uncomfortably cold after just a few moments. Once temperatures dip as low as 48 degrees, it is foolhardy to go swimming. Hypothermia can set in within the first thirty to sixty minutes, resulting in exhaustion and unconsciousness. The expected time of survival in water that cold is just one to three hours. The survival rate drops as the water temperature decreases.

George Hollands also wrote in his account of the collision that he was among the first to jump from the *Massachusetts* onto the deck of the *Black Diamond* as it swung around. Once on board, he realized that it was severely damaged and that he had "jumped out of the frying pan into the fire." In running toward the stern, he grabbed a stepladder off the hurricane deck, hoping it would help keep him afloat once he went overboard. At the last moment, it came to him "that the river was not deep enough to engulf the masts and all, so [he] threw down the ladder, grabbed one of the guyropes and began climbing up toward the mast." And so, he was saved.

According to the survivors, *Black Diamond* sank stern first, moments after the additional men got on board—in less than three minutes and in three and a half fathoms (twenty-one feet) of water, "creating a great dark hole in the water"[70] and leaving the cabin exposed above the surface of the river.

An article in the *Pittsburgh Daily Commercial* on April 27 reported that the *Massachusetts* succeeded in reaching Point Lookout safely despite its being crippled. Everyone disembarked there, and when the soldiers were all counted, they found that they were sixty-five men short. The steamer *Marion*, with Captain Mott, happened along and took on board some of the soldiers off the damaged *Massachusetts*, easing its load. Bound for Fort Monroe, Mott took these men there, arriving late Sunday night and leaving them to continue their journey south. Private Martin V. Culver, another survivor, wrote to his brother shortly after the accident to tell him that they finally reached Newbern on the following Saturday, April 29, 1865, after a long and hard passage.

Accident.—On Sunday night last there was a collision on the lower Potomac river, between the transport Massachusetts and the propeller Black Diamond, by which the latter vessel was so much injured that it sank immediately, with five or six men from the Quarter Masters' Department in this place, who were drowned. The steamer Massachusetts had on board some 300 soldiers for City Point, and, it is said, some 40 or 50 of these were knocked overboard when the vessels struck, and were lost.

Many newspapers of the day contained reports of the collision and the presumed number of dead, but bigger events in the news overshadowed this incident, causing it to be nearly lost to history. On April 21, President Lincoln's funeral train began its travels west, and its progress was being followed inch by inch in the newspapers. On the twenty-sixth, the hunt for the assassins ended when Booth and Herold were cornered in the Garret barn in Caroline County, Virginia. Booth was killed; Herold was captured and brought to the Washington Navy Yard. And then on the twenty-seventh, the steamer *Sultana* exploded in the Mississippi River, resulting in the loss of 1,167 lives. George Hollands recalled, "We watched the New York papers a few days following the accident for an account of it, but I never saw any mention of it. In those days, however, the loss of a ship and a few men was not considered worth mentioning."[71]

Of the men aboard the *Black Diamond*, six were initially reported as lost, but ultimately it was found that seven had drowned. Only four of their bodies were recovered. Those four were Peter Carroll, Christopher Farley, George W. Huntington and Samuel Gosnell. The other three who lost their lives have not yet been identified.

The survivors of the *Black Diamond*'s crew included the engineer, Joseph Husted, who wrote a report of the incident in 1874.[72] He tried to claim a pension in August 1890 but was turned down by the Quartermaster Department, as were the other civilian employees.

Compiling a list of the names of the men lost on the *Massachusetts* is much more difficult, as they came from so many different regiments. Inquiries were made of the government as early as 1925 in an effort to find a complete list, but none was ever found. Regulations stipulated that all passengers be listed by name when being transported, so it can be assumed that a list did exist at

The bodies of three the firemen connected with the United States Steam Fire Department, in this city, recently lost by the collision on the Potomac, which sunk the steamer Black Diamond, have been recovered and brought to this place. They will be buried this evening, at 4 o'clock, the procession to move from the Steam Engine House. The Fire Department, government and city, are to unite in the funeral ceremonies.

Opposite: The collision was reported in newspapers all across the country, but the press soon lost interest due to other bigger stories. *Alexandria Gazette*, April 26, 1865.

This page, top: The four men from the Union Steam Engine House were buried in the Alexandria National Cemetery. Theirs were four of the thirty-seven bodies that were recovered. *Alexandria Gazette*, May 10, 1865.

This page, left: Of the eighty-seven men known to have drowned in the collision, only thirty-three have been identified thus far. *Photo by W.E. Stone.*

one time. Of the eighty known to have drowned from the *Massachusetts*, only twenty-nine have been identified thus far.

The other fifty-four men who perished are not missing in the traditional sense. Some of their bodies were recovered and sent home. Some still lay on the bottom of the Potomac River. They did not go home, but they are now home. And they are remembered, even if we do not yet know their names.

CHAPTER 7

THE AFTERMATH AND INQUIRY

From what I can learn, the cause of the disaster was extreme carelessness of the pilot or master of the Massachusetts.
—letter from Assistant Quartermaster Captain J.G.C. Lee, Alexandria Depot, to U.S. Army Brigadier General D.H. Rucker, Quartermaster General, April 25, 1865

In the immediate aftermath of the incident, the death toll as stated in the newspapers was estimated to be about fifty men drowned; the final count was eighty-seven. On April 25, Brigadier General Daniel Rucker, quartermaster, Washington Depot, wrote to Captain E.S. Allen, assistant quartermaster, Washington Depot, that he had "directed that a steamer in charge of an officer with a party of men and extra small boats be sent immediately to Blackstone [*sic*] Island and vicinity to endeavor to recover the bodies of the men lost and bring them to Alexandria." Captain Allen dispatched the steamer *Charleston* to the scene the following day.

The steamer Charleston has been for some time engaged in looking for the bodies of those drowned by the sinking of the Black Diamond off Blackiston's Island. Thirty-seven bodies have been recovered and taken to Point Lookout. It has been ascertained that 87 persons perished with the Black Diamond.

Captain E.S. Allen, assistant quartermaster, Washington, D.C., sent search vessels to the site of the incident to recover the bodies of those men lost. *Alexandria Gazette*, May 6, 1865.

Armed with hooks, their mission was to search for and retrieve bodies of those supposed to be lost. They stayed in the area until May 12.[73] A gunboat was also stationed near the site of the wreck, and other Quartermaster Department vessels also assisted in the rescue effort, including the propeller steamer *Fannie*. The search and recovery efforts were greatly hindered by high water that spring.

The *Washington Evening Star* newspaper reported on May 1:

> *All efforts thus far to recover the bodies of the soldiers drowned in the Potomac river, by the sinking of the propeller* Black Diamond, *which was run into off Blackistone's Island a few days ago by the steamer* Massachusetts, *have been unsuccessful owing to the high water in the river. The number of lives lost by the sinking of the vessel has not been definitely ascertained as yet, but it is believed that at least sixty persons were drowned. The* Black Diamond *is entirely submerged in water, with the exception of her smokestack and the upper part of her pilot house. She will doubtless be a total loss, as she is an old vessel, and would not hold together if attempts were made to raise her.*

On May 4, the steamer *James Guy*[74] was heading up the Potomac and came across the site of the incident. Captain Fair reported that he saw several bodies of drowned men near Blackistone Island, whom he supposed to have been victims of the collision.[75] In all he saw five bodies, one without a coat and wearing a shirt and vest. The man appeared to be stout, with black hair. The others he could not in any way identify, as they were wearing coats, the capes of which were covering their heads. The captain went on to say that a gunboat was stationed near the island that he assumed was picking up and burying the bodies.[76] The next day, Captain Beaston of the steamer *J.W. Everman* reported passing a dead body floating in the water about a half mile below where the wreck occurred.[77] On May 11, the *Evening Star* reported that the steamer *Charleston* had been engaged in looking for the bodies of those drowned since the sinking of the *Black Diamond* and that only thirty-seven bodies had been recovered.

Since this incident fell under the marine risk clause, the U.S. government took no responsibility for it, laying it all at the feet of the owners. Although it was impossible at first to determine where the blame for the disaster lay, Captain Lee, assistant quartermaster, had no doubt. In his letter to the quartermaster general on April 25, he said, "From what I can learn the cause of the disaster was extreme carelessness of the pilot or master of the

Bodies Recovered.—A gun boat has been stationed at the place where the steamer Black Diamond was sunk, near Blackistone's Island, and her crew have succeeded in recovering more than twenty five of the bodies of those who were drowned. Captain Fair, of the steamer James Guy, bound up the Potomac on the morning of the 4th, saw several bodies of drowned men, which he supposed to have been victims of the late disaster to the Black Diamond, a few days since.

Only thirty-seven bodies were ever recovered. *Alexandria Gazette*, May 12, 1865.

Massachusetts." In a second letter penned later that same day, he reported the loss of sixty-six men and recommended that both captains and both pilots be arrested and brought to trial. Brigadier General Rucker and Secretary of War Stanton both agreed. Captain Meredith of the *Black Diamond* was arrested and held at the Central Guard House in Washington, D.C., which was used to house citizens and others who were charged with military offences. Meredith remained there until May 6, when he was released with a written parole, requiring him to appear whenever needed, presumably at the inquiry of the Board of Steamboat Inspectors. The charges were based on the rules laid out by the Thirty-Eighth Congress:

> *Thirty Eighth Congress. Sess. I, CH 69. 1864*
> *REGULATIONS FOR PREVENTING COLLISIONS ON THE WATER*
> *NO SHIP UNDER ANY CIRCUMSTANCES TO NEGLECT PROPER PRECAUTIONS*
> *Article 20. Nothing in these rules shall exonerate any ship, or the owner, or master, or crew thereof, from the consequences of any neglect to carry*

> *lights or signals, or of any neglect to keep a proper lookout, or of the neglect of any precaution which may be required by the ordinary practice of seamen, or by the special circumstances of the case.*

This was not without precedent. The legal responsibility of captains, pilots, engineers and other persons employed on any steamboat for loss of life occasioned by their misconduct, negligence or inattention to duty was first recognized in the Steamboat Act of 1838. This act recognized that with the increasing number of steamboats traveling on the inland waterways, the number of accidents was also increasing. So in 1838, the federal government created the Steamboat Inspection Service and charged it with three roles: the inspection of hulls, machinery and equipment of vessels; the licensing of officers and the certification of crews on those vessels; and the conduct of trials and investigations to ascertain violations of steamboat laws, rules and regulations. A very brief set of operational rules and regulations was also created at that time. These inspectors had no enforcement authority. Seeing that vessels complied with the rules and regulations of navigation and operation fell to the officers of the Customs Service, the forerunners of the United States Coast Guard.

By the act, the local federal district court judge was to appoint at least one inspector for each port, who was to be in charge of inspecting and certifying steam vessels operating there. And the task of investigating alleged acts of incompetency or misconduct committed while acting under the authority of licenses issued by the steamboat inspectors was given to these same local boards. The act empowered them to summon before them any witnesses within their districts and to compel their attendance by a process similar to that used by the district courts. If their investigation led them to conclude that the licensed officer was either incompetent or guilty of misconduct, negligence or unskillfulness, or had willfully violated any provision of the steamboat inspection laws, they were to revoke his license immediately.

The 1838 act also stated that vessel operators could be charged for criminal manslaughter for deaths resulting from misconduct or negligence aboard vessels in United States waters—a risk the government was unwilling to undertake. It said, in part, that "every captain, engineer, pilot or other person employed on board of any steamboat or vessel propelled in whole or in part by steam, by whose misconduct, negligence or inattention to his or their respective duties, the life or lives of any person or persons on board said vessel may be destroyed, shall be deemed guilty of manslaughter, and upon conviction thereof before any circuit court in the United States, shall be sentenced to confinement at hard labor for a period of not more than ten years."[78] Vessel owners and public officers were added to the list of those who could be held criminally liable with the passage of the Steamboat Act of 1864.[79]

It is a unique law in a sense because it made these deaths federal crimes rather than state crimes. It also varied from common-law manslaughter in that it required only simple negligence, such as a breach of duty to perform an act or omission in violation of a standard of care, not malicious intent. This was established as precedent during a case tried in 1848.[80]

Accidents continued, so in 1852, Congress passed an amendment to the Act of 1838 that included tougher regulations, established a system for their implementation and gave the steamboat inspectors authority to investigate all maritime accidents and violations involving casualties. The Steamboat Act of 1852 also moved the regulation and responsibility for steamboat inspections from the Department of Justice to the Department of Treasury, headed by Secretary Thomas Corwin.

Nine inspection districts were created, with one supervising inspector appointed by the president of the United States to oversee each one. These nine men reported directly to the secretary of the treasury. Local inspectors within each of these federal districts were appointed by a commission consisting of the local collector of customs, the supervisory inspector and the district judge.

Experience showed that the majority of the accidents had been caused by boiler explosions and shipboard fires, so a new category of inspectors was created to examine and certify hulls and boilers and to license steam engineers and steam pilots. The actual inspection requirements and the wording of the certificates were standardized at this time as well, ensuring uniform compliance with the rules.

According to the state laws of Maryland and Virginia, pilots were responsible for the safe navigation of vessels on the rivers in the Chesapeake Bay region, and no vessels were to travel these waters without a pilot on board. The duties of the pilots were codified in Maryland in 1787, although they were mentioned in the colonial records as early as the 1640s. The Act of 1852, quoted following, now made this a federal requirement and made the pilots subject to the regulations in it.

> *Whereas it is necessary for the safety and preservation of vessels bound from this state to sea or coming into Chesapeake Bay and bound up any river of this state, and to some port thereof, that able and experienced pilots*

> *should be established to conduct and pilot such vessels, for reasonable fees, to their several moorings, and that ignorant and unskillful persons should be prevented from undertaking such pilotage.*

The steamboat pilot certificates showed the pilot's name and rating, along with the required oath, which said that the signer would comply with the Congressional Act of 1852 regarding the supervision of steamboats and their machinery. By signing the oath, they certified their understanding and agreement. It was the pilot's responsibility to safely navigate the vessel in his charge up and down rivers and in and out of harbors. Beginning in 1852, these were federal certificates, issued through the local customs districts. Prior to then, each state had appointed its own examiners and provided its own regulations and certifications. Before receiving his certificate, each pilot was examined by the inspectors for his knowledge of the specific waterway he intended to sail, as well as his overall qualifications. Each license was valid for one year.

Like the pilots, the steam engineers underwent examinations and were licensed for a single year at a time. Once certified, they were to supervise the maintenance and operation of the steamboat's machinery. Each was rated by class, according to the size of the engines.

In 1852, the board also laid out a set of rules in relation to signals of sounds and lights for vessels, differentiating between ocean transport and river transport. This act was overturned by a federal legislative act in 1864 that instead simplified the rules, making one set valid for both ocean and river transport. Two of the Steamship Board's chief concerns with the new law were the requirement that mast lights be used (since few river steamers have masts) and the disallowing of the use of steam whistles as signals when approaching and passing other vessels. The new law also required headlights on the stern or other low position toward the bow, which the board argued caused confusion on rivers since they are generally on the same level as shore lights and landing lights and would therefore not be recognized as another vessel. The showing of red and green lights to indicate port and starboard was considered necessary only when a vessel was underway.

In his annual report of 1865, P.B. Stillman, president of the National Board of Inspectors of Steam Vessels, reiterated the board's concerns about the changes to the rules they had laid out in 1852. He argued that the new laws, as written by Congress, were going to make traveling the rivers and other inland waters of the United States unsafe—again. He stated that the rules for ocean travel and river travel needed to be different and even suggested that the Act of 1864 should be confined to just ocean travel. He argued that the system of lights and signals that had been in use since 1852 eliminated misunderstandings between vessels as they approached each other, thereby making travel safer. On the inland waters, mast headlights were impracticable, as no masts were used on those vessels. Headlights on the stern or other low position forward gave pilots a false aspect to the surface of the water, making it impossible for them to determine the channel or snags in their way. Nor could these low lights be distinguished from shore lights, so they should not be required. Stillman concluded his report with a statement of important occurrences brought to the board's attention in 1865. It shows:

Steamers inspected: 2,270 (includes Black Diamond *and* Massachusetts*)*
Pilots licensed: 3,172 (includes those serving on Black Diamond *and* Massachusetts*)*
Engineers licensed: 4,035 (includes those serving on Black Diamond *and* Massachusetts*)*
Violations of the law investigated: 28 (includes Black Diamond *and* Massachusetts*)*
Total number of lives lost: 2,560 (includes the 87 lost from the Black Diamond *and* Massachusetts*)*

At the time of the collision, the *Black Diamond* was at anchor so was not showing the red and green running lights. It was without a mast so had the one required headlight burning. The *Massachusetts* had the running lights showing, as it was underway, but was not allowed to use the steam whistle, which might have alerted the crew of the *Black Diamond* to its presence.

The Third Supervising District of Inspectors of Steam Vessels (Baltimore) held an inquiry into the *Black Diamond/Massachusetts* incident and submitted their findings to the National Board of Inspectors in October 1865 as part of their annual report to the secretary of the treasury. James N. Muller Sr., supervising inspector Third District, reported that the board's investigation found that both pilots "wholly disregarded the rules established for their government, consequently their licenses were revoked." He also reported that the local board was of the opinion that "this lamentable loss of human life has been caused by the present system of carrying signal lights."[81]

Assistant Quartermaster Allen recommended to Quartermaster General Rucker that the *Massachusetts* be discharged from military service due to its age; this was done at midnight on June 10, 1865. It was sold to the Individual Enterprise Steamboat Company of Baltimore, sent to the shipyard of

Messrs. Hazen & Company in Baltimore in October and given a thorough overhaul, including a new boiler. The *Baltimore Sun* reported that it would be ready to resume regular trips to the Eastern Shore by mid-November and "will be one of the finest steamers out of the port for winter service, having comfortable berths for one hundred and fifty passengers."[82]

CHAPTER 8

THE FINAL DISPOSITION

She will doubtless be a total loss, as she is an old vessel, and would not hold together if attempts were made to raise her.
—Washington, D.C. Evening Star, *May 1, 1865*

Sadly, the majority of the victims were never recovered, making it difficult for their families to prove their deaths. The *Evening Star* of May 11 stated that thirty-seven bodies had been recovered and taken to Point Lookout. A number of them were returned to their families for burial in their hometowns. Others, whose bodies were not recovered, were memorialized on monuments and other markers back home.[83]

The four men serving on the *Black Diamond* whose bodies were recovered were brought to Alexandria for burial. Their comrades felt they deserved the honors shown to others who died in the line of duty, so they petitioned for these four civilians to be interred in the Alexandria National Cemetery, which was under the control of the Quartermaster Department. Their petition was granted, and the men were buried in the federal cemetery on May 10, 1865, after a procession from the U.S. Steam Engine House to the cemetery. The fire department, the federal government and the city authorities all collaborated on the funeral arrangements.

A memorial was placed in their honor by fellow members of the Government Steam Engine Company in November 1865.[84]

Their graves (numbers 3174, 3175, 3176 and 3177) were originally marked by wooden markers, but in 1878, Joseph Weis, who had served with them,

> A monument has been erected in the Soldier's Cemetery in this place, by the members of the Government Steam Engine Company, over those of their company, who were lost from the steamer Black Diamond, near Blackistone's Island, in the Potomac, last April.

This page, top: The four men were buried in individual graves in the Alexandria National Cemetery, and a marker was put up in their honor in November 1865. *Photo by W.E. Stone.*

This page, bottom: *Alexandria Gazette*, November 11, 1865.

Opposite: In 1955, the federal government replaced the deteriorated original tombstones at the Alexandria National Cemetery with four new markers. *National Archives and Records Administration.*

WAR DEPARTMENT
Q. M. C. Form No. 14
Revised Oct. 6, 1928

Interment in the Alexandria, Va. **National Cemetery**

To—The Quartermaster General, Washington, D. C.

NAME	RANK	COMPANY	REGIMENT OR VESSEL: Number	State	Arm	DIVISION, IF WORLD WAR SOLDIER
Carroll, Peter	Civilian	Employee	QMD	civil - separate type hdst		

DATE OF DEATH: Month	Day	Year	DATE OF INTERMENT: Month	Day	Year	GRAVE MARK: Section	Grave No.	REMARKS: Date of discharge and number of Pension Certificate, Disinterments, etc.
April	24	1865					3177	5 MAY 1955 2466987 GREEN MOUNTAIN MARBLE CO. WEST RUTLAND, VT.

Shipping point for headstones

REPLACEMENT

hdst deteriorated

Superintendent.

3—2560

(See Instructions on Reverse Side)

6 8 2 9 0 2 1 0 0 1 9

requested that they be replaced with marble military-style headstones, which was done.[85] In 1955, the federal government replaced these headstones, which were deteriorating, with new markers in the same design and shape as the originals.[86]

Clara Barton, who had served as a nurse throughout the war, was at Camp Parole, Maryland, during the spring of 1865, when the men who were on the *Massachusetts* were also there. She was there in her capacity as an official government correspondent, seeking information on soldiers whose whereabouts were unknown. She obtained permission from President Lincoln to serve in this capacity, as a way of furnishing information to families about their missing loved ones. With the help of a few paid assistants, Barton opened the Missing Soldiers Office in Washington in 1865 and began publishing "Rolls of Missing Men," which were published in newspapers across the country and contained instructions for anyone with information about their whereabouts to write to her. She was instrumental in compiling the first list of men who had died while at Andersonville Prison. A Joint Resolution of Congress was passed in 1866, granting Barton $15,000 in support of her work in finding missing soldiers. When she wrote her final report to Congress in 1869, she shared the number of inquiries received, letters mailed, circulars printed and men identified during the four years the Missing Soldiers Office had been in existence.[87] She concluded the report with a plea to Congress, asking it to make a declaration of death for all soldiers still missing and unknown so their families could finally have closure and could seek financial relief through the pension system.

Many of the widows and mothers of the men who drowned from the *Massachusetts* were ultimately able to receive pensions. In order to do so, those whose loved ones were not returned to them had to rely on the depositions of survivors who had witnessed the incident and drownings to prove that they had died. In some cases, the regimental officers were able to testify, even though they had not been on board. The mothers who had relied on the money sent home by their sons had to further prove that they had been dependent on the income. It was often the town postmistress who attested to that for them, having handled each of the letters home. Ministers were also called on to testify in the women's case, proving marriage and the birth of children.

The *Black Diamond* was never raised. The smokestack and upper pilot house remained visible above water for some time, but the vessel was too old and badly damaged to attempt recovery so was deemed a total loss. At the time of its loss, the *Black Diamond* was valued at $25,000 ($500,859.87 in 2024).

The *Massachusetts* was decommissioned by the federal government at midnight on June 10, 1865, and sold to the Individual Enterprise Company and put back into commercial service. Then in May 1869, it was sold to the Maryland Steamboat Company. It remained in passenger service until 1881, when it was abandoned.

The *Alexandria Gazette* reported that regular steamboat service on the Potomac River resumed in May 1865, and the town was happy to welcome "several of our old Maryland and Virginia friends who have come to town, as in the old times, to purchase supplies."[88]

The Potomac Flotilla was put out of service on July 31, 1865, when Commander Parker issued a General Order to the officers and men of his command. It said, "The war for the preservation of American liberty being at an end, the Potomac Flotilla, which took its rise with it and grew with its growth until it had become a fleet rather than a flotilla, this day happily ceases to exist."[89] The wharf at Cross Manor in St. Inigoes that had been built by the government on the land it was renting for use as the coal depot was sold back to the property owner, Caleb M. Jones, for $400 ($7,724 in 2024). Jones received $25 a month in rent ($482.75 in 2024) during the time the flotilla was using his property.

On December 26, 1865, Brigadier General D. Wise suggested to Major General M.C. Meigs, quartermaster general, that the poem "Ode Written at the Beginning of the Year 1746" (popularly known as "How Sleep the

Brave") be used in conjunction with any publication of the names of the soldiers lost in the collision of April 23, 1865.[90] The poem was written in 1746 by the English lyric poet William Collins.

How sleep the brave who sink to rest,
By all their country's wishes blest!
When Spring, with dewy fingers cold,
Returns to deck their hallowed mold,
She there shall dress a sweeter sod,
Than Fancy's feet have ever trod.

By fairy hands their knell is rung,
By forms unseen their dirge is sung;
There Honour comes, a Pilgrim grey,
To bless the turf that wraps their clay,
And Freedom shall awhile repair,
To dwell a weeping Hermit there!

During the First Session of the Thirty-Ninth Congress (December 12, 1865–July 28, 1866), the Committee on Naval Affairs presented a report relating to the inquiry as to whether pilots engaged in the gunboat or other naval service of the government (including the Potomac Flotilla) during the late war should have been treated and paid as officers during their terms of service. The committee found that since these men had not been injuriously affected by the war but rather had seen their business increase, they were owed nothing further.

In April 1888, P.M. Dunkle, of Toby, Pennsylvania, who was a private with the 103rd Pennsylvania Infantry Regiment and had survived the wreck, placed a note in the *National Tribune* saying that he "would like to hear from some comrade who was on board the side-wheeled steamer *Massachusetts* 23 years earlier, on that fateful night in April 1865." No replies to his request have been found.

In 2020, Civil War Trails installed a marker in recognition of the tragic collision of the *Black Diamond* and the *Massachusetts* on the mainland, just opposite Blackistone Island, on the grounds of the St. Clement's Island Museum. The museum holds a wreath-laying ceremony annually in April to honor the men whose lives were lost. Local divers are attempting to locate the remains of the *Black Diamond* on the bottom of the Potomac River, and the search for the names of the missing men continues.

APPENDIX A

THE FULL ACCOUNT OF THE GOLDSMITH RAID

Blackistone Island Light Station was built in 1851, with funds appropriated in 1848. A fifth-order Fresnel lens was installed in 1857. In 1860, Jerome McWilliams, the keeper throughout the war, was reprimanded for excessive use of his oil supply. It was reported on March 14 and the recommendation was that his pay be withheld until he showed good cause.

The excuse given by McWilliams was that his oil had been used up by the vessels in the flotilla, so he did not have any to use in the lantern. Two years later, in February 1862, Keeper McWilliams did send receipts showing that the flotilla had indeed been using his oil—but the question remains, what was he doing with all the extra oil in 1860? Supply depots for the flotilla were eventually established at Piney Point Lighthouse and elsewhere for coal, oil and other supplies, which reduced expenses for the flotilla and left lighthouse supplies intact.

Keeper McWilliams's problems continued when a complaint was filed against him by Master Pilot Robert Watter in 1862 because the light was not lit. Lieutenant Edward McCrea, commander of the Potomac Flotilla vessel *Jacob Bell*, also reported that the lamp was dark at that time. The Blackistone light went dark again in 1864 when it was set upon by Rebels who destroyed the lens and lantern and took all the oil. An official report of the raid was submitted by flotilla Commander Parker on May 21, 1864, to Gideon Welles, the secretary of the navy, from on board the USS *King Philip*, stationed in St. Mary's County. In it, Commander Parker wrote:

> *Sir, I have to report to the Department that on the night of the 19th instant 12 rebels, headed by a man named Goldsmith, landed in a small boat at Blakistone* [sic] *Island, and destroyed the lens and lamp and carried off 15 gallons of oil belonging to the lighthouse at that point, without doing further injury. I have requested Colonel Draper, commanding at Point Lookout, to station a guard at Blakistone Island, at Piney Point, and on board the light-ship off Smith's Point, during the time that the vessels of the Potomac Flotilla are required for the protection of the army transports at Aquia Creek, Belle Plain, and in the Rappahannock and for the convoying of vessels carrying prisoners of war to Fort Delaware and Point Lookout. And I am of the opinion that while there are so many rebel sympathizers in Maryland and on the eastern shore of Virginia none of the lighthouses there located are safe without a guard on shore to protect them. I have the honor to be etc.*

Colonel A.G. Draper, the commander of the District of Southern Maryland, replied from his headquarters at Point Lookout on May 21, 1864:

> *Commodore PARKER,*
> *I have sent a sergeant with 22 men to Piney Point, and a lieutenant to consult with you about Blackiston's* [sic] *Island. The cavalry detachment cannot be spared from Leonardtown.*
>
> *A.G. DRAPER,*
> *Colonel Thirty-sixth U.S. Colored Troops, Commanding*

Ultimately, Federal forces were sent to the island on a gunboat and patrolled that area until the war's end.

The news of the 1864 attack was carried in the Washington, D.C. *Evening Star*. It mentions fourteen men, not the twelve of Parker's report. Parker also reported a smaller amount of oil as having been removed:

> *RAID ON A LIGHT HOUSE. Last Thursday night a party of fourteen persons, two of whom were colored, came out from the Virginia shore, and watching their chance made a dash across the Potomac to Blackiston's* [sic] *Island, and going to the light house at that point they proceeded to destroy the lamp and lanterns, which they did most effectually. They also carried off about twenty-five gallons of oil, and started to carry off the keeper, Mr. Jerome McWilliams, but through the entreaty of his family he was allowed to remain.*

The party were led by a man named John Goldsmith, of Westmoreland County, Va., and the others are said also to belong to that locality. Goldsmith has lately made several small raids across the river, and a short time since he and his companions robbed a store on the Maryland shore, compelling the proprietor to carry some of the goods to their boats.

Since the destruction of the lantern a hand lamp has been used.

McWilliams family legend says that Goldsmith was convinced to not carry off the keeper by the wife of the keeper, Fannie McWilliams, who insisted they take her as well, so in the end they left both the family and the building intact. The legend says that the heroic keeper signaled the Federal forces at Point Lookout as soon as the Rebels left. (It is possible that he signaled one of the flotilla vessels, which then carried word to Point Lookout, but it was not possible for him to contact Point Lookout directly, as it was 26.5 miles downstream and there was no telegraph at the lighthouse.) The family also says the lamp was repaired and relit in a matter of moments; this does not match the official report, which notes the use of a handheld lantern in place of the broken pieces. The official records do show that the requests for repairs and replacements were submitted immediately, and the replacements were soon received.

Another legend, also passed down through the family, says that Goldsmith intended to destroy the entire lighthouse by burning it down or blowing it up but was thwarted by Jerome McWilliams, who knew Goldsmith and pleaded with him not to do it. Jerome claimed that his wife, Fannie, was with child, and moving her and putting her through the stress of losing her home would endanger both lives. The legend goes on to say that Goldsmith abandoned this part of the plan, destroyed just the lantern and lens, confiscated the oil and left.

Years later, in 1909, the keeper was Josephine McWilliams Freeman, Jerome's sister, who also ran the family's nearby hotel. She would regale out-of-town guests with heroic tales, including the one about the Goldsmith raid. Her version of the event was reported in *Summer Resorts*, a special section of the Sunday *Star*, Washington, D.C., dated "Coltons, Md., July 23, 1909":

Mrs. W. Freeman, the lighthouse keeper on Blackistone Island, takes a great deal of pleasure in showing visitors to the lighthouse a piece of lens shattered by a shot from a Confederate war vessel during the civil war. Her brother, John McWilliams [Josephine did not have a brother named John, so it is assumed the reporter made an error and meant Jerome],

> *refused to put out the light when ordered by the Confederate commander, and the light was extinguished by the shot from the war vessel.*
>
> *Mrs. Freeman has been the lighthouse keeper for thirty-two years, succeeding her brother.*

Captain Goldsmith's account of the raid differs from all these versions in some of its details. It was published as "On the Potomac in 1864" in the *St. Mary's Beacon*, having first been published in the *Warrenton* (VA) *Index*. Goldsmith's family was from St. Mary's County and owned Enfield on St. Patrick's Creek. Like so many others in the county, he also owned land on the Virginia side of the river at the time of the Civil War. It is likely that Keeper Jerome McWilliams and Captain Goldsmith knew each other well due to the closeness of Goldsmith's lands to Blackistone Island and the fact that Goldsmith had owned the island in 1836 and then sold it to Benjamin Gwinn Harris, who in turn sold it to the McWilliams family in 1845.

Captain Goldsmith stated in his account of the raid that he was accompanied by only four men, Lieutenant Tom Parker, Sergeant James Parker, J. Spalding and a "Negro" by the name of Lewis. Lewis had been persuaded to come along on the pretext that they were going to raid a few chicken houses on the Maryland side; when he discovered the real purpose of the raid, he had to be forcibly restrained from jumping into the Potomac and striking out for the Virginia shore.

Goldsmith's boat was thirty feet long and known as the *Swan*. Captain Goldsmith had operated many successful missions throughout the war, taking goods and men across the Potomac. On this night, he said they slipped past a Federal gunboat anchored near the island; wrecked the lamp and all the fixtures; carried off about two hundred gallons of oil, "which was very acceptable to the government at Richmond"; and took away the light tender. They had planned to dynamite the lighthouse, but the keeper, Jerome McWilliams, pleaded that his wife, who was expecting a baby and was near her time, would be endangered if moved, so they abandoned this part of the plan.

Throughout the years, some of the people in the area have said that the McWilliams family were secretly sympathetic to the Confederate cause, but even if they were, the keepers were all employees of the United States government and had sworn an oath when they took their post, agreeing to uphold the Constitution of the United States.

Near the end of the war, Captain Goldsmith was arrested and held as a prisoner of war at Point Lookout. Federal authorities had been looking for him since 1861, knowing he was associated with the men who had been captured after burning the lightships. In his account of the raid on the Blackistone Lighthouse, Goldsmith stated that the officers of the Potomac Flotilla had been promised "a handsome premium for the capture of the *Swan* as she was considered so troublesome to the Federal forces."

The inspector's report from September 1864 is, in contrast to the anecdotal stories, very precise about the repairs and renovations after the Goldsmith raid. A new lantern was put in place that was a more modern version of the old one. The porch was also added to the house at this time. When the inspector arrived to repair the lamp, he found everyone out sitting under a tree—the only shade they could find.

There were many other incidents at Blackistone Island during the war. Many vessels were stopped while passing in the vicinity and taken by the Potomac Flotilla for lack of passes, improper paperwork, questionable cargo and so on. Beginning in May 1863, the flotilla vessel *Eureka* was stationed at the island for the protection of the lighthouse, and in June, someone from the island hailed it and a small boat was sent ashore in response. The officer in charge captured seven men who were crossing from Virginia as refugees, with one being kept as a prisoner of war on suspicion of being either a deserter, a smuggler or a spy.

APPENDIX B

GENERAL ORDER NO. 276

WAR DEPARMENT,
No. 276

ADJUTANT GENERAL'S OFFICE
Washington, D.C. August 8, 1863

To secure and preserve discipline, provide against disaster from the elements or attack by the enemy, the Senior officer in the military service of the United States, present with troops upon any transport, will assume command, unless he finds, on going on board, a commander already designated by proper authority.

All troops on board the transport will, at the earliest moment after embarking, be inspected and organized into detachments or companies. The Senior Officer will assign officers to each detachment or company, and take all measures necessary to put his command into the best state of efficiency to meet any emergency.

This order applies to all troops on board of transports, whether on duty or furlough, or in separate detachments; and the Senior Officer on board will be held responsible for any failure in the performance of the duties above imposed upon him, and for the enforcement of his command of strict observance of the Article 37, Revised Army Regulations, for the government of troops and transports.

He will require, when arriving in sight of port, a report of the voyage from the Senior Officer or acting Officer of each Staff Department on board, and will transmit it with his own report, through proper channels, to the Adjutant General of the Army.

These reports should give any facts of interest touching the accommodation and health of the troops, the manner in which the officers and crew of the transport have performed their duties, and the length of the voyage, and any observations which may enable the War Department to correct abuses and punish neglect.

This order will be placed in a conspicuous position in every chartered or purchased transport.

By order of the Secretary of War:

E.D. TOWNSEND,
Ass't Adj't General

APPENDIX C

"THE COLLISION ON THE POTOMAC"

William H. Nott First Sergeant, Co. K. 16th CT
The National Tribune
Washington, D.C.
January 29, 1914

Editor National Tribune: About 350 of us, ex–prisoners of war, who had been recruiting* at Camp Parole, Annapolis, MD., after being in Andersonville and other prisons, were ordered to Alexandria, VA., to take a boat for Newbern, N.C., to join our different regiments and complete our term of service.

I do not remember what time in the evening it was that we took the steamer Massachusetts at Alexandria, but between 12 and 1 o'clock at night, as we were steaming down the Potomac in fine shape, there was a crash. The Black Diamond had crossed the bows of our steamer and received a blow just back of the wheelhouse, which cut a hole in her down to the water's edge. At the same time the Black Diamond carried off our bow, making a hole large enough to take in five or six men abreast, down to within a foot of the water's edge.

We were all sleeping on the deck and other places about our steamer. When the crash came both Captains called out at the same time, "We are sinking!" and all was confusion. The Captain of the Black Diamond saw that his boat was in worse shape than our steamer, and as he had only a crew of 17 he ordered the Black Diamond to swing around to the side of our steamer, and our Captain ordered us all into the stern of our boat to keep the bow up.

We all thought that the Black Diamond was a relief boat and our passengers commenced to jump onto her, and the more that jumped the quicker the Black Diamond went down. I stood on the side of our steamer and saw about 150 of my comrades jump down into the Black Diamond. About 55 or 60 were drowned that night, including seven of my regiment.

When the Black Diamond swung around she smashed one of our lifeboats, so that we had but one to pick up those in the water. Our steamer worked all night and picked up about 50. Claudius Margerum was in the water nearly three hours. He is yet living at Springfield, Mass.

In the morning we started for Newbern, N.C. We were mustered out at Newbern, June 24, 1865.

William H. Nott First Sergeant, Co. K. 16th Conn., Bristol, Conn.

*This is probably meant to be "recovering" rather than recruiting.

APPENDIX D

CHIEF ENGINEER HUSTED'S STATEMENT OF THE SINKING OF STEAMER *BLACK DIAMOND*

Joseph F. Husted, Chief Engineer, steamer *Black Diamond*
Philadelphia
May 20, 1874

Philad[a] May 20th, 1874

Statement of the sinking of Steamer Black Diamond in the Potomac River in the Year 1865

Steamer Black Diamond left Alexandria Virginia April 23rd, 1865 with Special Orders from Captain Allen, Quartermaster at Washington D.C. We took 1 Captain and 10 men to do Guard Duty on board, the 10 men belonged to the Volunteer Fire Department of Alexandria VA, some of them belonged to Easton P[a] and some belonged to Frankford Philad[a] City. We proceeded down the Potomac River to Piney Point. We left Piney Point at 11 O'clock P.M bound up the Potomac River. About 12[35] O'clock AM on the 24th nearly opposite Blackstone Island Lighthouse the side wheel steamboat Massachusetts ran into the steamer Black Diamond causing her to sink in about 8 minutes. The Massachusetts had on board several hundred Soldiers at the time bound for Fort Monroe. During the collision the soldiers on the Massachusetts became Panic stricken and jumped on the Black Diamond under the impression that the Massachusetts was sinking. The Crew of Steamer Black Diamond were all saved excepting Stewardess and 1 of the 10 Volunteers of the Alexandria Fire Department who were drowned. We afterwards ascertained that there was 86 in all lost. I do not know any of their names Excepting 1 Drummer Boy belonging to the 16th Connecticut Vol. he gave me his name (George J. Carter*) while I was Endeavoring to save him, but he was so benumbed that he could not catch hold of the line.

Yours Respectfully

Joseph F. Husted

Engineer Str. Blk Diamond

*The musician George Carter's middle initial is actually W.

APPENDIX E

"ON THE *MASSACHUSETTS*"

The Midnight Collision on the Potomac Between the *Massachusetts* and the *Black Diamond*.
George Hollands, Co. B. 101st Pennsylvania
The National Tribune
Washington, D.C.
May 14, 1914

Editor *National Tribune*: I was very much interested in the description of the collision on the Potomac in your issue of Jan. 29 by Comrade William H. Nolt, 16th Conn., which regiment was unfortunately captured at Plymouth, N.C., April 20, 1864, together with my regiment, the 101st Pa., two companies of heavy artillery, a company of cavalry and the 24th N.Y. Ind'p't Battery.

The whole brigade was taken to Andersonville, arriving there on May 1, 1864.

In September, on account of the close proximity of Sherman's army, we were removed to another prison, or "bull pen," as we called it, at Florence, S.C., and the following December, under a cartel of exchange effected between the Commissioners of exchange of both North and South, about 10,000 of those who were suffering most were paroled and taken to Camp Parole, Annapolis. We remained there until after the assassination of President Lincoln in April, 1865, when, as Comrade Nolt says, we were ordered to Alexandria, Va., to take a boat for the North Carolina Coast, where recruits had been sent to fill up our depleted ranks.

On Sunday, April 23, 1865, about 5 o'clock in the afternoon, about 400 of us boarded the steamer Massachusetts and started down the Potomac for Norfolk, Va.

We glided along down the river very nicely until a little after dark, when a strong wind began to blow and the river became very rough, and, as our boat was an old one and unfit to carry more than half the number she had on board, the outlook was not very encouraging. About 10 o'clock at night, when we were all cuddled down for a night's sleep, part on the upper deck and part below—myself and my bunkmates were stretched out on the lower deck—we heard an awful crash and felt a sudden jar. We all sprang to our feet, pulled on our coats and ran up on deck to see what the trouble was. All was confusion and excitement, as we discovered we had crashed into the side of another boat, striking her amidship.

I ran to the bow of our boat, as most of the others had done, and found her bow was settling fast. The Captain was shouting to us to go aft, so as to keep her bow out of the water as much as possible. In the meantime we were shouting to the boat we had run into—the Black Diamond—to come to our assistance. She circled around and came up alongside of us, and about 150 jumped from the Massachusetts to the deck of the Black Diamond. I was among the first to board her, and I ran immediately to the man at the wheel and asked him if the boat was all right. He said: "No; she is sinking." I then made up my mind that we had "jumped out of the frying-pan into the fire." I immediately turned to go toward the stern of the boat, and in going I stumbled onto a stepladder which had been torn from the hurricane deck. I grabbed up the ladder and was about to jump overboard with it—scores of the boys had already jumped overboard to avoid the suction of the boat as she went down—when all of a sudden the thought came to me that the river was not deep enough to engulf the masts and all, so I threw down the ladder, grabbed one of the guyropes and began climbing up toward the mast.

I soon landed my foot on the yard-arm and got my arms around the mast, and about that time the boat struck bottom, with her deck only about two feet under water. I found three or four of the crew among the rigging, so they evidently were of the same mind as I concerning the depth of the river. We clung to our positions all night and could hear the cries for help in all directions from the boys who had jumped overboard.

A drummer boy of the 16th Conn. had been washed overboard and had grasped hold of the keel of the boat, or something else, and was hanging on for dear life and calling for help. One of the crew up in the rigging got hold of a rope and time and time again threw it to where the boy was, telling him to grab for it. The boy couldn't get hold of it. Every now and then a wave would wash over him and strangle him, and as he would emerge from it he would call for the rope. He finally became exhausted and cried out to us that he could hold out no longer. He told us his name, but I have forgotten it. [George W. Carter] He said he was a drummer of Co. D, 16th Conn., and asked us to inform his mother that he was drowned. He bade us goodbye, and as the next wave washed over him he loosened his hold and sank beneath the waves.

We clung to our position until daylight, when we were discovered and picked up by a small United States gunboat or revenue cutter and transferred to our old boat, the Massachusetts, which, with one wheel out of commission and part of her bow carried away, had floated about in the vicinity during the night and picked up those she could of our comrades who had jumped overboard.

After we were safe onboard the Massachusetts made her way slowly down the river, and about 11 o'clock a.m. she sighted a large steamer lying at anchor. She steered for her and ran alongside, and we were immediately transferred to the larger boat.

In making the transfer we were counted off and were found to be 65 short. Our new boat at once steamed away for Norfolk, Va., arriving there about 4 o'clock p.m., where we were unloaded and sheltered in an old theater overnight. The next morning we were loaded on a small steamer and ran thru the canal to Roanoke Island, where we found the recruits that had been assigned to our different regiments.

In closing I wish to say that Comrade Nolt's article is the first and only mention I ever saw of it in print. We watched the New York papers a few days following the accident for an account of it, but I never saw any mention of it. In those days, however, the loss of a ship and a few men was not considered worth mentioning.

George Hollands, Co. B, 101st Pa., Hornell, N.Y.

APPENDIX F

LIST OF KNOWN DEAD, BURIALS AND MONUMENTS

Black Diamond Losses

Quartermaster Department
U.S. Steam Engine House, Alexandria, Virginia
Peter Carroll, Blacksmith
Buried in the Alexandria Federal Cemetery, Alexandria, Virginia
Christopher Farley, Carpenter
Buried in the Alexandria Federal Cemetery, Alexandria, Virginia
Samuel N. Gosnell, Blacksmith
Buried in the Alexandria Federal Cemetery, Alexandria, Virginia
George W. Huntington, Blacksmith
Buried in the Alexandria Federal Cemetery, Alexandria, Virginia

Massachusetts Losses

7th Connecticut Infantry Regiment, Company B
Private Charles W. Vibbert
Captured at Battle of Plymouth, North Carolina, April 1864; held prisoner at Andersonville, Georgia
No interment or memorial records found; presumed body was not recovered

16th Connecticut Infantry Regiment

Company B

Sergeant Samuel E. Grosvenor

Captured at Battle of Plymouth, North Carolina, April,1864; held prisoner at Andersonville, Georgia

Body not recovered; listed on Soldier's Monument in Guilford, Connecticut

Private Henry S. Loomis

Captured at Battle of Plymouth, North Carolina, April 1864; held prisoner at Andersonville, Georgia

Body not recovered; listed in War Memorial Building (GAR Hall) Vernon, Connecticut

Private Charles L. Robinson

Captured at Battle of Plymouth, North Carolina, April 1864; held prisoner at Andersonville, Georgia

Buried in Arlington National Cemetery, Arlington, Virginia

Company D

Corporal William T. Loomis

Captured at Battle of Plymouth, North Carolina, April 1864; held prisoner at Andersonville, Georgia

Body not recovered; cenotaph and military-issued marker in Enfield Street Cemetery, Enfield Connecticut

Musician George W. Carter

Captured at Battle of Plymouth, North Carolina, April 1864; held prisoner at Andersonville, Georgia

Body not recovered; cenotaph in West Suffield Cemetery, West Suffield, Connecticut

Company I

Private George N. Champlin

Captured at Battle of Plymouth, North Carolina, April 1864; held prisoner at Andersonville, Georgia

Body not recovered; name listed on the side of his brother Andrew's memorial in Old Springs Cemetery, Stafford Springs, Connecticut

Company K

Private Edward Smith

Captured at Battle of Plymouth, North Carolina, April 1864; held prisoner at Andersonville, Georgia

Body not recovered; listed as Lost at Sea on Civil War Memorial in West Cemetery, Bristol, Connecticut

1st Maine Heavy Artillery

Company F

Private John Hall

Hospitalized with incised wound and jaundice; Harewood Hospital, Washington, D.C.

No interment or memorial records found; presumed body was not recovered

Company H

Sergeant Augustus P. Nash

Captured at Battle of Weldon Railroad, Virginia (Petersburg Campaign), August 1864; held prisoner at Danville, Virginia

Body not recovered; listed on Nash family marker in Steuben Village Cemetery, Steuben, Maine

2nd Massachusetts Heavy Artillery

Company G

Private Charles Ayers

Captured at Battle of Plymouth, North Carolina, April 1864; held prisoner at Andersonville, Georgia

No interment or memorial records found; presumed body was not recovered

Company H

Private William H. Drury

Captured at Battle of Plymouth, North Carolina, April 1864; held prisoner at Andersonville, Georgia

No interment or memorial records found; presumed body was not recovered

Private John Philips

Captured at Battle of Plymouth, North Carolina, April 1864; held prisoner at Andersonville, Georgia

No interment or memorial records found; presumed body was not recovered

Private Charles F. Remmick

Captured at Battle of Plymouth, North Carolina, April 1864; held prisoner at Andersonville, Georgia

No interment or memorial records found; presumed body was not recovered

11th Massachusetts Volunteer Infantry Company D
Private William B. Foster
Captured at Battle of Hatcher's Run, Virginia (Petersburg Campaign), February 1865; held prisoner at Danville, Virginia
No interment or memorial records found; presumed body was not recovered

25th Massachusetts Volunteer Infantry Company H
Private Samuel F. Hall
Captured at Battle of Cold Harbor, Virginia, May 1864; held prisoner at Andersonville, Georgia
No interment or memorial records found; presumed body was not recovered

34th Massachusetts Infantry Company K
Private Joshua Phillips
Captured by John Singleton Mosby near Newtown, Virginia, November 1864; most likely held prisoner at Danville, Virginia
No interment or memorial records found; presumed body was not recovered

39th Massachusetts Infantry Company E
Sergeant Edward Ladd
Captured at Battle of Plymouth, North Carolina, April 1864; held prisoner at Andersonville, Georgia
No interment or memorial records found; presumed body was not recovered

59th Massachusetts Infantry Company B
Private Thomas Murphy
Captured (and wounded) at Battle of the Crater, Petersburg, Virginia, July 1864; held prisoner at Danville, Virginia
No interment or memorial records found; presumed body was not recovered

9th New York Heavy Artillery Company K

Private Anis Byron

Captured at Battle of Monocacy, Maryland, July 1864; held prisoner at Danville and Richmond, Virginia

No interment or memorial records found; presumed body was not recovered

Private Jerome W. Gardner

Captured at Battle of Monocacy, Maryland, July 1864; held prisoner at Danville and Richmond, Virginia

No interment or memorial records found; presumed body was not recovered

Private William Harrington

Captured at Battle of Monocacy, Maryland, July 1864; held prisoner at Danville and Richmond, Virginia

No interment or memorial records found; presumed body was not recovered

93rd New York Volunteers Company B

Private William F. Roycroft

Captured at Battle of Deep Bottom Run, Virginia (Petersburg Campaign), July 1864; held prisoner at Andersonville, Georgia

No interment or memorial records found; presumed body was not recovered

94th New York Volunteers Company E

First Sergeant John R. Fitzgerald

Captured at Battle of Weldon Railroad, Virginia (Petersburg Campaign), August 1864; held prisoner at Danville, Virginia

No interment or memorial records found; presumed body was not recovered

45th Pennsylvania Regiment Company A

Private Philip Parient

Captured at Battle of Peebles' Farm, Virginia (Petersburg Campaign), September 1864; held prisoner at Danville, Virginia

No interment or memorial records found; presumed body was not recovered

101st Pennsylvania Infantry Regiment Company H
Wagoner Jeremiah Bale
Captured at Battle of Plymouth, North Carolina, April 1864; held prisoner at Andersonville, Georgia
No interment or memorial records found; presumed body was not recovered

Private Henry J. Friday
Captured at Battle of Plymouth, North Carolina, April 1864; held prisoner at Andersonville, Georgia
No interment or memorial records found; presumed body was not recovered

118th Pennsylvania Infantry Regiment Company E
Private Cunningham Johnston
Captured at Cold Harbor, Virginia, June 1864; held prisoner at Andersonville, Georgia
Buried in North Cedar Hill Cemetery, Philadelphia, Pennsylvania

140th Pennsylvania Volunteer Infantry Regiment Company F
Private William Krepps
Captured at Battle of Cold Harbor, Virginia, May 1864; held prisoner at Richmond, Virginia; transferred to Andersonville, Georgia
No interment or memorial records found; presumed body was not recovered

APPENDIX G

LETTER FROM JOSEPH E. WEISS TO SECRETARY OF WAR GEORGE McCRARY

Philadelphia
January 20th, 1878

Hon. Geo W. McCrary Secretary of War
Dear Sir

There [are] four bod[ies] lying in the national cemetery at Alex Va. Their names are Geo Huntingdon Peter Carroll Samuel Gosnell & Christian Farley. They were Employed in the Quartermasters Dept at Alex Va [Alexandria, Virginia] during the Rebellion when our beloved President was Assassinated in April 1865, they Volunteered with others to patrol the Potomac River in Search of the Assassins on board of the Propeller Black Diamond. I not remembering the date of the month in the night time the transport Massachusetts going to City Point loaded with troops run into the Black Diamond and Sunk her & these four men drowned with Some of the troops We there Comrades & fellow Workmen had there bod[ies] bought to Alex Va & with permission of the Government there bod[ies] interred in the National Cemetery at that place & had a monument Erected there for them We have Understood that there was Some of the Appropriation left that was appropriated for Marble head Stones We now ask Your Hon if You Could place four Stones at the heads of these men If So I Will get the States that they are from or Mr. Davis Having charge of the Cemetery

In 1878, friends of the four men from the Union Steam Engine House sent a letter requesting that some of the appropriations for military headstones be used to mark the graves of their comrades Peter Carroll, Christian Farley, Samuel Gosnell and George Huntingdon. *Photo by W.E. Stone.*

can do it by So doing You Will confer a great favor to Many of their old Comrades hoping to hear from you when convenient I being Selected to Send this note to You

Please Address
18 Police Dist. Phila Pa

I Remain Fraternally
Jos E Weiss

APPENDIX H

TIMELINE OF THE CIVIL WAR

1842

Black Diamond built by Hogg & Delamater for use on the Delaware and Raritan Canal.

Massachusetts built for service in Nantucket.

1861

APRIL

12: Fort Sumter fired on.

15: President Lincoln calls for troops.

17: Virginia secedes from the Union.

19: Baltimore draft riots lead to Maryland being placed under Federal military control.
President Lincoln confiscates all four of the Richmond, Fredericksburg & Potomac Railroad (RF&P) Company's steamers for use by the Union as troop transport vessels.

19–24: Two light vessels in the Potomac River are burned by the Confederates (Upper and Lower Cedar Point).
Buoys and channel markers are also destroyed.

20: Virginia takes control of the RF&P property at Aquia Creek, Virginia, and sends Confederate engineers to design a defensive position there; General Ruggles is then given command of the batteries.

22: James Ward proposes the formation of the Potomac Flotilla.

27: Plan for the flotilla approved, with Ward in command.
29: Maryland's first vote on secession fails to pass.

MAY

29: Potomac Flotilla sees its first action in the Battle of Aquia Creek.

JUNE

27: Commander James Ward (head of Potomac Flotilla) killed during Battle of Mathias Point (first naval officer killed during Civil War).

AUGUST

16: President Lincoln issues Proclamation 86, which prohibits commercial trade with states in rebellion.

SEPTEMBER

One-third of Maryland's state legislators are arrested by Federal troops under Butler, preventing the secession vote.

OCTOBER

17: Potomac River is declared closed by Federal authorities due to blockade by Confederate shore batteries.

NOVEMBER

20: Lafayette Baker takes troops to Southern Maryland to deal with disloyal postmasters.

1862

National Board of Inspectors of Steam Vessels establishes rules in relation to signals, differentiating between ocean transport and river transport.

MARCH

9: Potomac River is reopened after Confederates abandoned the shore batteries.

JULY

System of prisoner parole and exchange devised.
Camp Parole established near Annapolis, Maryland.

DECEMBER

Black Diamond chartered by the Quartermaster Department.

1863

APRIL

All prisoner exchanges halted.

JUNE

31: Martial law declared in Baltimore and all counties on the Western Shore of Maryland.

AUGUST

General Order No. 276 issued, requiring Veteran Reserve Corps to serve as officers of troop transport vessels.

OCTOBER

14: *Massachusetts* chartered by the Quartermaster Department.

DECEMBER

31: Commander Foxhall Parker takes over as the head of the Potomac Flotilla.

1864

1862 rules for steamboat signals overturned by federal legislative act.

APRIL

20: Battle of Plymouth, North Carolina, where many of the men on the *Massachusetts* are captured.

MAY

19: Goldsmith Raid on Blackistone Lighthouse.

Flotilla begins to maintain a gunboat patrol around the island perimeter until the war ends.

JUNE

Light vessels at Upper and Lower Cedar Point replaced by this time with new vessels.

JULY and AUGUST

The siege of Petersburg, Virginia, where many of the men on the *Massachusetts* are captured.

NOVEMBER

1: New Maryland state constitution takes effect, abolishing slavery in the state.

DECEMBER

Plymouth prisoners paroled and sent to Camp Parole near Annapolis, Maryland.

1865

SPRING

Clara Barton, working at Camp Parole, begins the work that leads to her creation of the Missing Soldiers Office.

APRIL

3: Confederate capital of Richmond falls.

9: Confederate General Robert E. Lee surrenders to Union General Ulysses S. Grant.

14: President Lincoln assassinated by John Wilkes Booth.

15: Orders sent by Colonel F.D. Sewall, district commander, that no trains, vessels or boats of any kind are to leave Annapolis.

Booth and his accomplice David Herold stop in Charles County, Maryland, at the home of Dr. Samuel Mudd so that Booth's broken leg bone can be set.

17: Orders sent to Potomac Flotilla to search all vessels going out of the river for the assassins.

19: Parker orders all boats traveling on the Potomac be seized.

21: Reports received that Booth and Herold have been seen in St. Mary's County.

Booth and Herold attempt to cross the Potomac but end up back on the Maryland shore.

22: Lafayette Baker and his force board steamer *Ide* to head to Port Conway and pick up trail of assassins.

Booth and Herold successfully cross the Potomac, arriving on the Virginia shore the morning of the twenty-third.

Three hundred soldiers march out of Camp Parole heading to Alexandria, Virginia, to be transported south to rejoin their regiments.

23: *Black Diamond* receives special orders to join the Potomac Flotilla.

Massachusetts leaves Alexandria, Virginia, at 5:00 p.m., carrying troops south to rejoin their regiments.

24: The crash occurs just before 1:00 a.m., sinking *Black Diamond* and damaging *Massachusetts.*

Lafayette Baker sends Theodore Woodall with a telegraph operator into lower Maryland to enable communication with that region without loss of time.

25: Quartermaster General Rucker dispatches a steamer to recover bodies.

Captain Lee, assistant quartermaster, Alexandria Depot, blames the pilot or master of *Massachusetts* for the wreck and calls for the arrest of both captains and both pilots.

26: John Wilkes Booth is killed; David Herald is captured; both are taken to Washington, D.C.

29: Survivors of the wreck reach Newbern, North Carolina.

JUNE

10: *Massachusetts* discharged from government service and returned to passenger service duty.

JULY

31: Potomac Flotilla leaves the Potomac River (orders to disband were received on the seventeenth).

OCTOBER

25: Third Supervising District of Inspectors of Steam Vessels holds inquiry and revokes both pilots' licenses.

NOVEMBER

11: Boulder and plaque for men lost from the *Black Diamond* erected at Alexandria National Cemetery.

1866

AUGUST

20: President Andrew Johnson formally declares an end to the Civil War.

1867

Veder Fox given permission to raise a number of vessels in the Rappahannock and other rivers, but not *Black Diamond.*

1869

Clara Barton writes her final report to Congress, including a plea that a declaration of death be given for all soldiers still missing and unknown so their families can obtain their pensions.

1881

After being sold twice, *Massachusetts* is abandoned; final disposition unknown.

1890

AUGUST

Joseph Husted, *Black Diamond*'s chief engineer, attempts to claim a pension.

1914

JANUARY

29: William Nott's account of the incident appears in the *National Tribune*

MAY

14: George Hollands's account of the incident appears in the *National Tribune*

1955

NOVEMBER

New headstones placed on the graves of the four men lost from the *Black Diamond*

2015

APRIL

St. Clement's Island Museum holds the first commemorative ceremony (it becomes an annual event in 2018)

2020

NOVEMBER

Civil War Trails installs an interpretive panel about the wreck on the grounds of the St. Clement's Island Museum, on the mainland near St. Clement's (Blackistone) Island

NOTES

Chapter 1

1. Thomas H. Hicks to Simon Cameron, April 20, 1861, *War of the Rebellion: Union and Confederate Armies*, I:1, ix, 442.
2. Letter from Daniel M. Thomas to "My Dear Sister," April 21, 1861, *The Papers of Daniel M. Thomas, 1674–1938*, MS 1970.2, Maryland Center for History and Culture.
3. Henry Winter Davis to Colonel William Turnbull, December 25, 1860, Turnbull Collection, MS 1719, Maryland Center for History and Culture.
4. Davis, *Speeches and Addresses Delivered in Congress*, January 2, 1861, 189–90.
5. *Frederick Herald*, November 28, 1860.
6. *St. Mary's Beacon*, March 7, 1861.
7. Abraham Lincoln to Winfield Scott, April 25, 1861, Roy P. Basler, *The Collected Works of Abraham Lincoln*, vol. 4:3444.
8. *Baltimore Sun*, April 29, 1861.
9. *St. Mary's Beacon*, August 30, 1861, 2.
10. According to the Official Register of the United States, 1861, there were nine post offices authorized to operate in St. Mary's County, but one, at St. Clement's Bay, had discontinued service on December 6, 1860.
11. Telegram to secretary of state from L.C. Baker, October 10, 1861.
12. Baker, *Spies, Traitors & Conspirators*, 108–17.
13. Baker, *Spies, Traitors & Conspirators*, 122–23.
14. The first commander of the flotilla, James H. Ward, was killed in action off Mathias Point on June 27, 1861. Thomas T. Craven took his place and served until December 1861.
15. Citizens of St. Mary's County to Commander Thomas Craven, Commanding Potomac Flotilla, July 21, 1861.

16. Commander Harwood served as the commander of the Potomac Flotilla from September 1862 through December 1863.
17. Report of Lieutenant Commander Magaw, U.S. Navy, senior officer Potomac Flotilla, to Commodore A.A. Harwood, commandant Navy Yard, Washington, D.C., August 11, 1862.
18. Major O'Beirne had been captain of the Thirty-Seventh New York Infantry, but after being severely wounded at the Battle of Chancellorsville in May 1863, he was mustered out and recommissioned as captain in the Veterans Reserve Corps in July. He was promoted to the rank of major in July 1864 and, beginning in April 1865, was serving as the provost marshal of Washington, D.C.

Chapter 2

19. Report of Activities by Ed L. Haines, commander U.S. steamer *Rescue*, to Navy Yard, September 30, 1861, Potomac Flotilla Microfilm Records, National Archives: Potomac Flotilla Records: Microfilm M89A: Entry 45: Rolls 114–16.
20. *Alexandria Gazette*, May 13, 1861.
21. Report of commandant Navy Yard Washington, regarding replacement of buoys on Kettle Bottom Shoals, April 27, 1861; Order of the secretary of the navy to commandant Navy Yard Washington, D.C., regarding replacement of buoys, April 27, 1861. *War of the Rebellion: Official Records of the Union and Confederate Navies*, series I, volume IX, 431.
22. Report of June 15, 1861, from Flotilla Commander Ward onboard flotilla steamer *Freeborn* to Secretary of War Gideon Welles, National Archives: Potomac Flotilla Records: Microfilm M89A: Entry 45: Rolls 114–16.
23. Letter from Secretary of the Treasury to Shubrick, September 12, 1862, National Archives Record Group 26, Entry #24, Box 1: Letters Received 1861–63.
24. Lighthouse Service Book of Letters, 5th District Engineers and Inspectors, National Archives Record Group 26, Box 165, Entry #24.
25. Letter to Lieutenant R.H. Wyman, commanding Potomac Flotilla, from Gideon Welles, secretary of the navy, December 16, 1861, reporting on statement made by Captain Shore of the steamer *Chamberlin*, Potomac Flotilla Records: Microfilm M89A, Entry 45: Rolls 114–16.
26. Now known as St. Clement's Island.
27. Near the end of the war, Captain Goldsmith was arrested and held as a POW at Point Lookout Prisoner of War Camp. Federal authorities had been looking for him since 1861, knowing he was associated with the men who had been captured after burning the lightships.
28. For a complete account of the attack on the Blackistone Lighthouse, see Appendix A.
29. Telegram of June 9, 1861, from onboard the USS *Resolute*, National Archives: Potomac Flotilla Records, microfilm, M89A: Entry 45: Rolls 114–16.
30. National Archives, Potomac Flotilla Records: Microfilm M89A: Entry 45: Rolls 114–16.

Chapter 3

31. Steamers are classed according to tonnage and construction. Propellers of 350 tons or over are assigned to the first class; those of about 250 tons to the second class; and those of 150 tons or less to the third class. Sidewheel steamers are given a lower classification than propellers of like tonnage.
32. *Vulcan*, *Ironsides* and *Anthracite.*
33. $1 in 1862 is equivalent to $31.17 in 2024; in 1863, $24.98; in 1864, $20.05; and in 1865, $19.31.
34. These were the first twin-screw steam vessels in the country.
35. Every steam vessel carried a certificate of inspection that stated the number of passengers it could safely carry. If this number was exceeded, there were financial penalties for the ship's master or owner.
36. *Baltimore Sun*, May 1861.

Chapter 4

37. *War of the Rebellion: Official Records of the Union and Confederate Armies*, series 1, vol XLVI, pt. 3, 754, 756, 769.
38. Hard, *History of the Eighth Cavalry Regiment*, 320–21.
39. Telegram, Navy Department, April 17, 1865, from Secretary of Navy Gideon Welles to Foxhall Parker, Commanding Officer of Potomac Flotilla, St. Inigoes, Maryland, National Archives: Potomac Flotilla Records: Microfilm M89A: Entry 45: Rolls 114–16.
40. Telegram, Navy Department, April 17, 1865, from Secretary of Navy Gideon Welles to Commanding Officer of Naval Force, Hampton Roads, Virginia, National Archives: Potomac Flotilla Records: Microfilm M89A: Entry 45: Rolls 114–16.
41. Report from Foxhall Parker, USS *Don*, to Gideon Welles, secretary of the navy, July 31, 1865, National Archives: Potomac Flotilla Records: Microfilm M89A: Entry 45: Rolls 114–16.
42. Herold rode away from Seward's house when a servant ran out into the street yelling, "Murder!" leaving Powell to fend for himself. Herold met up with Booth as planned, but Powell was picked up later that night at Mary Surratt's boardinghouse—one of the only places in the city he knew. Both were ultimately hanged for their roles in the conspiracy.
43. Jones, *John Wilkes Booth*, 98–101.
44. *Juniper* was purchased at New York City from Solomon Thomas on June 7, 1864, and commissioned at New York Navy Yard on July 11, 1864. *Juniper* arrived at the Washington Navy Yard on July 17, 1864, and two days later was attached to the Potomac River Flotilla, where it served during the remainder of the war.
45. Log of the USS *Juniper*, National Archives, Records of the Bureau of Naval Personnel, Record Group 24.
46. Normal operations resumed on April 27, the day after Booth was killed and Herold was in custody. National Archives: Potomac Flotilla Records: Microfilm M89A: Entry 45: Rolls 114–16.

Chapter 5

47. In April 1863, the Alexandria City Fire Department reported that only two of the four volunteer fire companies were capable of meeting emergencies. Two engines had been destroyed and the companies disbanded. The remaining two steam fire engines, housed on Princess Street, were being operated by the U.S. Army Quartermaster Department and responded to fire alarms in the city until the war's end.
48. Robert Kellogg Diary, Connecticut Museum of Culture and History, MS68013.
49. Blakeslee, *History of the Sixteenth Connecticut Volunteers*, 90.
50. Blakeslee, *History of the Sixteenth Connecticut Volunteers*, 97.
51. Robert Kellogg Diary, Connecticut Museum of Culture & History, MS68013.
52. Hollands, "Andersonville Memories."
53. Diary of Samuel E. Grosvenor, Company B Sixteenth Connecticut Volunteers, Connecticut Museum of Culture and History, MS 81588.
54. Cooper, *In and Out of Rebel Prisons*, 218.
55. Moss, *Annals of the U.S. Christian Commission*, 319.
56. Diary of Samuel E. Grosvenor, Company B Sixteenth Connecticut Volunteers, Connecticut Museum of Culture and History, MS 81588.
57. *National Republican*, December 6, 1864, 1.
58. Robert Kellogg to Comrade Whitney, October 15, 1909, Connecticut Museum of Culture and History, MS 68013.
59. See Appendix B for full text of order.

Chapter 6

60. Telegram, Navy Department, April 17, 1865, from Secretary of Navy Gideon Welles to Foxhall Parker, commanding officer of Potomac Flotilla, St. Inigoes, Maryland, National Archives: Potomac Flotilla Records: Microfilm M89A: Entry 45: Rolls 114–16.
61. Ordered by Lieutenant Commander Eastman, U.S. Navy, Point Lookout, Washington, D.C., April 22, 1865, National Archives: Potomac Flotilla Records: Microfilm M89A: Entry 45: Rolls 114–16.
62. Diary of Henry Whittington, April 22, 1865, Special Collections of the Alexandria Public Library, Alexandria, Virginia.
63. The moon was waning and nearly gone, with only 8.67 percent of the moon face lit when it was in the night sky. By this time that night, the moon had set and was approximately 50 degrees below the horizon.
64. Newbern is the Northern spelling used at the time; the correct spelling is New Bern.
65. Nott, "Collision on the Potomac." See Appendix C for the complete article.
66. Pension Records of Anis Byron, deposition by George Peckham, April 7, 1866, National Archives Pension Files.
67. Banks, *Hidden History of Connecticut Union Soldiers*, 154.
68. See Appendix D for the full text of the statement.

69. Hollands, "On the Massachusetts." See Appendix E for the complete article.
70. Banks, *Hidden History of Connecticut Union Soldiers*, 155.
71. Hollands, "On the Massachusetts." See Appendix E for the complete article.
72. See Appendix D for the full text of the statement.

Chapter 7

73. *Alexandria Gazette*, May 12, 1865.
74. This steamboat had been seized and put into service by John Gillis, commander of the vessel *Pocahontas*, on May 21, 1861. National Archives: Potomac Flotilla Records: Microfilm M89A: Entry 45: Rolls 114–16.
75. "Bodies Recovered," *Alexandria Gazette*, May 6, 1865, 3.
76. "Bodies Found," *Daily Constitutional Union*, May 6, 1865.
77. "River News," *Washington Chronicle*, May 5, 1865, 2.
78. Twenty-Fifth Congress, Sess. II, CH. 191, July 7, 1838, 304, www.govinfo.gov.
79. Thirty-Eighth Congress, Sess. I, CH. 249, July 4, 1864, 390–92, www.govinfo.gov.
80. The seaman's manslaughter law is still used today, most recently in a 2023 case in California involving a fire on a dive boat, in which the captain was found guilty by way of negligence.
81. Stillman, "Report of the Supervising Inspector of Steamboats."
82. *Baltimore Sun*, October 26, 1865, 1.

Chapter 8

83. See Appendix F for list of burial and monument locations.
84. *Alexandria Gazette*, November 11, 1865, 3.
85. See Appendix G for the full text of the letter.
86. U.S. Department of Veterans Affairs, "The Black Diamond Crew and the Hunt for John Wilkes Booth," department.va.gov/history/featured-stories/052-black-diamond.
87. The Missing Soldiers Office received 63,182 inquiries, wrote 41,855 letters, mailed 58,693 printed circulars, distributed 99,057 copies of the printed rolls and identified 22,000 men. National Park Service, "Memorial of Clara Barton, Praying," www.nps.gov/museum/exhibits/clba/exb/Work/Office_of_correspondence/CLBA46_letterFront.html#:~:text=It%20is%20Clara%20Barton's%20report,the%20families%20to%20receive%20compensation.
88. *Alexandria Gazette*, May 29, 1865.
89. General Order of Commander Parker, U.S. Navy, commanding Potomac Flotilla, to the officers and men of his command on the disbanding of the flotilla, USS *Don*, July 31, 1865.
90. Letter from Brigadier General D. Wise to Major General M.C. Meigs, December 26, 1865, in the Special Collections of the Alexandria Public Library, Alexandria, Virginia, Quartermaster Records, Box #089, Folder M, Document #9.

SELECTED REFERENCES

Newspapers

Alexandria Gazette, Alexandria, Virginia
Baltimore Sun, Baltimore, Maryland
Congressional Globe, Washington, D.C.
Daily Constitutional Union, Philadelphia, Pennsylvania
Evening Star, Washington, D.C.
Frederick Herald, Frederick, Maryland
Hartford Courant, Hartford, Connecticut
The National Tribune, Washington, D.C.
New York Times, New York, New York
South, Baltimore, Maryland
St. Mary's Beacon, Leonardtown, Maryland
Washington Chronicle, Washington, D.C.

Official Regimental Histories, Accessed Online

7th Connecticut Infantry
16th Connecticut Infantry
85th Connecticut Infantry
1st Maine Heavy Artillery
2nd Massachusetts Heavy Artillery
9th New York Heavy Artillery
101st Pennsylvania
118th Pennsylvania Volunteers
3rd Regiment Veteran Reserve Corps

Government Records at the National Archives and Records Administration

"Annual Report of the Quartermaster General of the Operations of the Quartermaster Department to the Secretary of War for year ending June 30, 1865."

Military Pension Records

Potomac Flotilla Files

Quartermaster Department Files

Records of the Bureau of Naval Personnel

Records of the Lighthouse Service

"Report of the Secretary of the Treasury on the State of Finances for the Year 1865."

Stillman, P.B., president. "Report of the Supervising Inspector of Steamboats." October 1865. As found in *Report of the Secretary of the Treasury on the State of the Finances for the Year 1865*. Washington, D.C.: Government Printing Office, 1865.

Government Records, Accessed Online

25th Congress, Session II. www.govinfo.gov.

38th Congress Session I. www.govinfo.gov.

39th Congress, Session I. www.govinfo.gov.

Andersonville Prison Records. CivilWarPrisoners.com.

Military Pension Records. Fold3.com.

Published Firsthand Accounts

Hollands, George. "Andersonville Memories." *National Tribune*, September 27, 1906.

———. "On the Massachusetts." *National Tribune*, May 14, 1914.

Nott, William H. "The Collision on the Potomac." *National Tribune*, January 29, 1914.

Manuscripts

Diary of Henry Whittington. Alexandria Public Library.

Diary of Oliver W. Gates. Connecticut Museum of Culture and History.

Diary of Samuel E. Grosvenor. Connecticut Museum of Culture and History.

Papers of Robert Kellogg. Connecticut Museum of Culture and History.

Papers of the Loper Family. Library of Congress.

Turnbull Collection. Maryland Center for History and Culture.

Books

Baker, Lafayette. *Spies, Traitors & Conspirators of the Late Civil War*. Philadelphia: John E. Potter & Company, 1884.

Banks, John. *Hidden History of Connecticut Union Soldiers*. Charleston, SC: The History Press, 2015.

Basler, Roy P. *The Collected Works of Abraham Lincoln*. New York: Abraham Lincoln Association, 1953.

Bates, Samuel P. *History of Pennsylvania Volunteers, 1861–5*. Harrisburg, PA: B. Singerly, State Printer, 1871.

Blakeslee, Bernard F. *History of the Sixteenth Connecticut Volunteers*. Hartford, CT: Case, Lockwood and Brainard Co., 1875.

Brown, George William. *Baltimore and the Nineteenth of April 1861*. Baltimore, MD: Johns Hopkins University Press, 2001.

Bryan, George S. *The Great American Myth*. Chicago: Americana House, Inc., 1990.

Cooper, Alonzo. *In and Out of Rebel Prisons*. Oswego, NY: R.J. Oliphant, 1888.

Davis, Henry Winter. *Speeches and Addresses Delivered in the Congress of the United States, and on Several Public Occasions by Henry Winter Davis of Maryland.* New York, 1867.

Dyer, Frederick. *A Compendium of the War of the Rebellion*. Des Moines, IA: Dyer Publishing Company, 1908.

Floyd, Claudia. *Union Occupied Maryland.* Charleston, SC: The History Press, 2014.

Gibson, Charles Dana. *Dictionary of Transports and Combatant Vessels, Steam and Sail, Employed by the Union Army, 1861–1868*. Camden, ME: Ensign Press, 1995.

Gordon, Lesley J. *A Broken Regiment: The 16th Connecticut's Civil War.* Baton Rouge: Louisiana State University Press, 2014.

Hard, Abner. *History of the Eighth Cavalry Regiment, Illinois Volunteers During the Great Rebellion*. Aurora, IL, 1868.

Jampoler, Andrew J. *The Last Lincoln Conspirator*. Annapolis, MD: Naval Institute Press, 2008.

Jones, Thomas A. *John Wilkes Booth*. Chicago: Laird & Lee Publishers, 1898.

Mills, Eric. *Chesapeake Bay in the Civil War*. Atglen, PA: Schiffer Publishing, 2010.

Moss, Lemuel. *Annals of the United States Christian Commission*. Philadelphia: J.B. Lippincott & Co., 1868.

Schlotterbeck, John T., Wesley W. Wilson, Midori Kawaue and Harold A. Klingensmith, eds. *James Riley Weaver's Civil War.* Kent, OH: Kent State University Press, 2019.

Steers, Edward, Jr., ed. *The Trial*. Lexington: University Press of Kentucky, 2003.

Swinton, William, and Thomas Nast. *History of the 7th Regiment, National Guard, State of New York during the War of the Rebellion…1833–1892*. New York: Nabu Press, 2010.

Wills, Mary Alice. *The Confederate Blockade of Washington, D.C. 1861–1862*. Parsons, WV: McClain Printing Company, 1975.

———. *The War of the Rebellion: A Compilation of the Official Records of the Union and Confederate Armies in the War of the Rebellion.* Washington, D.C.: Government Printing Office, 1880–1901.

———. *The War of the Rebellion: A Compilation of the Official Records of the Union and Confederate Navies in the War of the Rebellion* Washington, D.C.: Government Printing Office, 1880–1901.

INDEX

ABOUT THE AUTHOR

Karen Stone has been the museum division manager for St. Mary's County, Maryland, where this event took place, since 2017. She did her undergraduate work at Gettysburg College and obtained her master's degree at Penn State University. When in fourth grade, she announced that she was going to be a museum director when she grew up. She got her first museum job while still in middle school and has been working in the museum field ever since. She has been a Lincoln fan and student of his assassination since childhood, so she was fascinated when she first heard this story with its connection to Lincoln and John Wilkes Booth. She was surprised to find it had been overlooked by history, which was enough to get her started on learning more and making sure the world would not forget again.

This is the first book for Stone, but she has published many articles and has been a frequent lecturer on U.S., state and local history.

Stone lives in Fredericksburg, Virginia, with her husband, and they have one adult son who is married and living in Alexandria, Virginia. In her spare time, Stone sings with the Chamber Chorale of Fredericksburg and at as many Fredericksburg Nationals baseball games as she can.